COME,
TAKE MY HAND

Follow Me

RSI
PUBLISHING

Dennis L Taylor

Cover Design By Roy Anderson

Scriptures are taken with permission from the New International Version of the Bible

Books may be ordered through booksellers or by contacting:
Dennis L Taylor
luke252.dennis@gmail.com

ISBN: 9781960641366

Printed in the United States of America
Edition Date: December 2023

Table Of Contents

Special Thanks

I want to thank Roy Anderson for his friendship and willingness to be used by God. We go back to the late 80s when we played Church League softball against each other. There has always been mutual respect for our playing abilities. Years passed, and both our playing days were over and done; God brought us back together unexpectedly. From the years of playing ball and living life, God did massive work in our lives. I think we both had to learn about dying to self and fully living for the Lord.

When God reunited us, we were both different men in Christ. We sat down at Cracker Barrell in Albany, Georgia, and spent the next two hours discussing how good God has been to us both. I told Roy how the Lord took one of my greatest fears and turned it into my greatest passion. I shared with him my love for writing and my desire to encourage others. I didn't know what he would say or think, so I told him I wanted to write a devotional called Fuel for Today. I waited for him to crack a joke or rag me about writing. To my surprise, he thought it was great and encouraged me to pursue my dream. Boy, was I surprised! Then Roy asked me what I imagined the cover would look like. So, I told Roy my vision for the cover, and he smiled.

To my surprise, Roy was an artist. Who would have ever expected that? Who would have ever thought two old ball players from way back would team up to get a book published? The only One not surprised was God. Seeing how God will use us if we surrender everything to Him is fantastic. He designed the cover for my first book, and now

Roy willingly permitted me to use one of his latest paintings for my newest devotional, "Come, Take His Hand."

Roy, thank you again for everything you do and your encouraging spirit. You are a blessing to so many people. Keep shining and using your talent for the glory of the Lord. I am looking forward to what God is going to do. It is great to be on the same team! You are still hitting long home runs. Love you, my brother.
Dennis

-1-
The Struggle

Years ago, I read a story about an old fisherman who came to town every Saturday afternoon. He always brought his two dogs with him. One was white, and the other was black. He had taught them to fight on command. So, every Saturday afternoon in the town square, the people of this little town would gather, and these two dogs would fight, and the fisherman would take bets. The white dog would win on Saturday, but the black dog would win the next two Saturdays. But the old fisherman always won! His friends began to ask him, "How do you do it?" He said, "I starve one and feed the other. The one I feed always wins because he is stronger." I know that isn't kind, but it's an excellent illustration for today.

> Ephesians 6:12 says, "For our struggle is not against flesh and blood, but against the rulers, against the authorities, against the powers of this dark world and against spiritual forces of evil in the heavenly realms."

So, we know our world has spiritual forces seeking to keep us from God and doing His will. But we must not blame Satan for everything that goes wrong or every sin we commit. Often, it is our sinful nature that is at work within us. We have two natures within us, both struggling for control. Here is my question for you today: which one dominates you? It depends on which one you feed. If you feed the spiritual nature and allow the Holy Spirit to empower us, He will rule over you. The flesh will dominate us if we starve the spiritual nature and feed that old sinful nature.

> *Galatians 5:17-18 says, "For the sinful nature desires what is contrary to the Spirit, and the Spirit what is contrary to the sinful nature. They are in conflict with each other, so you do not do what you want. But if you are led by the Spirit, you are not under the law."*

The battle goes on inside of us. The good news is this: if you are in Christ Jesus, you have been set free from the law of sin and death. Sin no longer reigns, but it still fights. When we receive Jesus as our Lord and Savior, we are blessed with the gift of the Holy Spirit. He is there to break old habits, purify our motives, set our eyes on new goals, and give us the desire to be more like Christ in everything we say and do.

> *First John 4:4 says, "Greater is He who is in you than he who is in the world."*

That is good news for you and me today. Yes, there will always be that struggle in our lives, but we must know that Jesus will give us the power to resist temptation. Because of the blood of Jesus, we can overcome. "Thank you, Lord!" No matter what you are struggling with today, know there is hope in Jesus Christ. The Holy Spirit will give you everything you need to experience victory over sin and death. But pay close attention to what nature you feed as you walk through this life. God bless you today; stay strong.

-2-
How's Your Run?

Psalm 32:1-4 says, "Blessed is he whose transgressions are forgiven, whose sins are covered. Blessed is the man whose sin the Lord does not count against him and in whose spirit is no deceit. When I kept silent, my bones wasted away through my groaning all day long. For day and night, your hand was heavy upon me; my strength was sapped as in the heat of summer."

Sin weighs us down, and for some reason, we decide to carry it around in our infinite wisdom and hang on to it for a while. It's like running a 5k race; you approach the starting line and, at the last minute, decide to return to your car and put on your ankle weights. The race is about to start, and you return to the line just in time to start your run. The gun goes off, and you take off. One hundred yards into the race, you begin to realize you made a bad mistake putting on the ankle weights, but pride won't allow you to stop and take them off. So, you keep pushing yourself and make it to the first thousand feet, but you are worn out. You are tired and defeated; you feel like you are giving up, and all your energy is sapped from your body. Let's go back and see what David said in Psalm 32:5:

"Then I acknowledged my sin to you and did not cover up my iniquity. I said, 'I will confess my transgressions to the Lord'-and you forgave the guilt of my sin."

In other words, David took off the ankle weights in this race called life. He got his heart right with the Heavenly Father, and he confessed his failures, and God saved him from the guilt and the pain. Don't allow selfish pride to keep you from getting your heart right with God. That heavy load of sin will catch up with you, open your spiritual eyes to truth today, and seek God's face. Without seeing the depth of sin, we will never understand the height of God's grace and love.

Take time to pause today and notice what is weighing you down. What sin are you carrying around with you twenty-four hours a day? Is guilt flooding your soul? Maybe you are drowning in depression and loneliness. It's time to take those ankle weights off and confess your sins to a loving God. Today is the day to walk in freedom and righteousness. I was always told, as a child, that it's not how you start the race, but it's all about how you finish. So, let God strip you of those ankle weights; you will be surprised by how much faster you can run. So confess your sins today, drop that heavy load, and let's finish strong for the glory of God. Amen.

-3-
His Little Was More Than Enough

Mark 6:1-10 says, "Jesus crossed to the far shore of the Sea of Galilee, and a great crowd of people followed him because they saw the miraculous signs he had performed on the sick. Then Jesus went up on a mountainside and sat down with his disciples. The Jewish Passover Feast was near. When Jesus looked up and saw a great crowd coming towards him, he said to Phillip, "Where shall we buy bread for these people to eat?" He asked this only to test him, for he already had in mind what he was going to do. Phillip answered him, 'Eight months' wages, would not buy enough bread for each one to have a bite!' Another of his disciples, Andrew, Simon Peter's brother, spoke up, 'Here is a boy with five small barley loaves and two small fish, but how far will they go among so many?' Jesus said, 'Have the people sit down.' There was plenty of grass in that place, and the men sat down, about five thousand of them."

Don't you love how Jesus messes with Phillip's mind? We all know the story; this was one of the great miracles of Jesus. Five thousand men were there that day, but we know they were not alone. Women and children covered the hillside, wanting to see and hear Jesus that day. There could have been around fifteen thousand people in the middle of nowhere with nothing to eat except this little boy with five barley loaves and two fish. Let me go off-script for a second. Do you mean out of fifteen thousand people there that day, only one little boy had food? Think about it; some moms had to be there with a few sandwiches. There had to be some dads there who carried the leftover meatloaf with them that day. This boy was so insignificant that he was even mentioned in the five thousand men count. But he willingly gave all he had to Jesus. It wasn't enough to feed this crowd, but he gave it anyway.

> *John 6:11-13 says, "Jesus then took the loaves, gave thanks, and distributed to those who were seated as much as they wanted. He did the same with the fish. When they had all had enough to eat, he said to his disciples, 'Gather the pieces that are left over. Let nothing be wasted.' So they gathered them and filled twelve baskets with the pieces of the five barley loaves left over by those who had eaten."*

Have you ever felt so insignificant and wondered how you could make a difference? You may feel like this little boy in this scripture, knowing other people probably had more to give, but that didn't stop him from giving his all to Jesus. What he had wasn't much, but in the hands of the Savior, it was more than enough to feed fifteen thousand people. Be encouraged today; God loves to use ordinary people to do extraordinary things. So look up; God is working behind the scenes of your life, and make sure to do the little things well each day. God has a way of promoting those who are faithful and willing to give Him everything. If God can do a crazy miracle with this little boy's lunch, what could he do with you? Dare to dream today.

-4-
A Prayer For Strength

Ephesians 6:10 says, "Be strong in the Lord and His mighty power."

When I read this verse, my spirit led me to think about the warfare of a Spirit-filled believer. How many of us are beat up and tired today? A spiritual battle is happening around us, and we are at war.

Ephesians 6:12-13 tells us, "For our struggle is not against flesh and blood, but against the rulers, against the authorities, against the powers of this dark world and against the spiritual forces in the heavenly realms. Therefore, put on the full armor of God, so that when the day of evil comes, you may be able to stand your ground."

I believe, with all my heart, that prayer is what pushes back the work of Satan. He can't stand it when the Church drops to its knees to pray to the Heavenly Father. He hates it when we praise the Lord for His goodness. He can't stand it when we stop long enough to thank Jesus for giving his life. Think about it: why do you think a prayer meeting is one of the least attended services of the local church? The devil works extra hard to keep the Christians far from prayer meetings. That is why I want to encourage you to pray this prayer today. I encourage you to pray out loud. Pray: Father, guard my eyes; help me to be aware of Satan's schemes. Please help me see the sneak attack on my life and my family's life before it happens. Please help me to move forward today with my spiritual eyes wide open. Lord, strengthen my grip; help me to hold tight to your Truth. Please give me the strength and the toughness to embrace your Word and never let it go. Use the resistance I face in this life to make me stronger. Please don't allow me to wallow in self-pity. When hard times come, please help me to keep going and not back down. Keep reminding me that these tough times are preparation for what you have called me to do.

"Heavenly Father, build up my endurance, get my heart rate up with a passion for You. Please help me to take a deep breath during tough times and give me the courage to trust you fully. Shield the wind as I run with you, and set my pace at a speed that is pleasing to you. Please fill me with wisdom today, and help me listen to my instructor, the Holy Spirit that lives inside me. Thank you, Lord. Amen."

Ephesians 6:11 says, "Put on the full armor of God so that you can stand against the devil's schemes."

Get ready for the battle today. If you are unaware of the fight around you, you probably get your butt kicked spiritually. So I want to close with Ephesians 6:18, "Pray in the Spirit on all occasions with all kinds of prayers and requests. With this in mind, be alert and always keep praying for all the saints."

Yes, I want to push you to pray today for yourself, but I also challenge you to pray this prayer over someone in your family. Let me know how it goes. God bless.

-5-
My Prayer And Thoughts

I want to start our devotion today by opening up with a prayer. Ensure you are away from all distractions, that your mind is set on the Father, and that you are ready to receive from Him today. Pray this prayer slowly, and as you pray, imagine you are looking into the face of God. I felt led today to share the prayer with the Father.

Heavenly Father, invade the space of my heart today; come and take over. I willingly kick myself off the throne of my heart and take your rightful seat, which is the throne of my life. I lay my sins at your feet; cleanse me and remove the guilt and the shame. Empty me of selfishness and pride, and give me a heart like Jesus. Lord, open my eyes to see things like you know every situation. Please open my eyes to see people around me, not with a spirit of judgment, but let me see them with glasses of compassion. Please help me see every situation that comes to me as an opportunity, not a burden.

Lord, give me ears to hear your voice, allow me to be sensitive to the voice of the Holy Spirit, and then give me the courage to be obedient no matter the cost. Let my hands and feet be a helpful tool to serve other people as you open the doors of ministry. Keep my body healthy so I can help you all the days of my life.

Lord, fill my mind with godly thoughts, dreams, and visions with your Word, and give me creative ways to give it away. Help me today to identify the lies of Satan and help me see his snares before I walk up on them. Then give me wisdom that only comes from you.

Lord, fill me with passion, fill me to the point of overflowing, and allow it to spill out on everything and everyone I touch. Thank you, Lord, for listening. Thank you, Lord, for the gift of the Holy Spirit. Thank you, Lord, for godly friends and mentors. I bless your Holy name today. Amen. Amen.

A couple of years ago, God led me to start sharing a few lines of my time alone with Him with my friends. It didn't make much sense to me, but I wanted to walk out what he told me to do. I don't know what I will share most days, so I open my Bible and wait for Him to lead me. I discovered that God has a new word for me every day and that new word encourages me and guides me through that day. It gives me energy, passion, and the desire to fulfill my calling.

I'll put it differently: The best bread is fresh bread. Some days, God will even cover it with a lot of butter. In my simple mind, I figured if it encourages me, it may inspire others.

In the last ⅓ of my life, I have been called to inspire people. I don't know what the last ⅓ of my life will look like, where I will be, or what position I will hold. But I do know what I will be doing; I am called to be a Barnabas, a son of encouragement. I want to encourage you to open up daily with time alone with God. Reading books by godly men and women is good, but fresh bread is the best. Follow your dreams and passions, and allow God to lead and guide you.

Remember this: be patient and wait on Him because He has everything worked out. Then, when He is ready, be ready to jump and take a leap of faith because the jump changes everything.

One of the godliest men I know said this recently, and it grabbed me, "The miracle is in the jump. It takes great faith on both sides of the miracle."

James 1:22 says, "Don't merely listen to the word, and so deceive yourselves. Do what it says." Walk out what God is telling you to do. No, it will never be easy, but He blesses obedience.

-6-
O My Goodness

My brother-in-law and mentor, Billy Durham, wrote a prayer guide for our church to help us to have focused prayer for twenty-one days. Today closes out those twenty-one days, and I want to share the simple but powerful prayer we pray as a Church today. Billy wrote; Lord, would you send an awakening to our community? I pray that we will see thousands of people come to know you. Give me more compassion and love for those around me who do not have a relationship with you, and give me the courage to live my life the way the Bible says to live my life. Amen.

That prayer stirred up the Holy Spirit in my soul, questions began to pop up about our community, and questions about "The Church" not a church, began to roll through my head. Questions like, are we loving our brothers and sisters in Christ in a way that pleases Him? They are edifying and encouraging each other to keep running and pushing forward. Are we cheering each other on and earnestly praying for each other? Do we see the needs of the people that are hurting and alone? Do we, as Christians, take time to look around and see people who are desperate for love and crying out for help as we live our lives? Is there unity in your community of believers? The questions kept coming, and I couldn't turn them off. It was like trying to sip water from a fire hydrant. I already felt overwhelmed by this first set of questions. But the Holy Spirit kept moving and stirring up the pot. More questions began to bubble and surface in my spiritual eyes. Questions like: Do we as

Churches have a genuine concern for those caught in addictions, young families struggling to put food on the table for their kids, and those whose eyes are empty of hope? Are we about the Kingdom of God or an earthly reign? I don't know if that was the awakening Billy was talking about, but that woke me up like a bucket of ice water.

Father, I pray that you will awaken the community of churches where I live. Open our eyes to see our sins and pride. Bring unity, bring oneness, and cover us in your love. Cover us with your anointing, protect us with your power, and help us walk out what we believe. I also pray that the community will give us an open door to their lives and a willingness to hear the message of Jesus Christ. Today, I pray for the thousands of people coming to the Lord this year in my community. I am trusting you for that miracle of LIFE. Father, give us a spirit of boldness, the words to say, and a heart of compassion. Lord, do something in this city that we have never seen before. Help us to break out of the four walls of a building and carry Jesus everywhere we go. Wake us up, Lord. Amen. Today, don't roll right past all these questions. I challenge you to write them down on another sheet of paper, then answer each one. What is God saying to you today? Are you awake yet? God bless your time of worship today.

-7-
Share Truth Today

We all have those times when we must tear down the walls we have allowed to exist. We all fall short, and we all mess up. But having a God who understands and shows us so much grace is good. Thank you, Lord, for the gift of forgiveness and mercy. Thank you for lifting me and encouraging me daily! Thank you, God, for the privilege to come before you when I need to say, "I am sorry." Thank you for tearing down that old wall of sin in my heart. Yes, be thankful, but this is just the beginning of what God has for us as children of God. Not only does God want to break down the old walls of our lives, but He also wants us to build a solid foundation. A foundation that is solid and will stand firm even when the worst storms come our way.

> *Matthew 7:24-25 Jesus says, "Therefore everyone who hears these words of mine and puts them into practice is like a wise man who built his house on the rock. The rain came down, the streams rose, and the winds blew and beat against that house; yet it did not fall, because it had its foundation on the rock."*

What is your life built on?

Before I go any further, I want to ensure you have a personal walk with Jesus Christ. Has there been a time in your life when you have come face to face with Jesus? Have you had an encounter with the Living God of the universe?

Being a Christian and a Christ follower isn't about our church attendance. It is not about doing good deeds or being morally good. It's about a personal relationship with Jesus and making Him the foundation for everything. Jesus suffered, bled, died on a rugged cross, and was buried. But Jesus didn't stay in that grave! I have hope, knowing that Jesus overcame sin and death. Thank you, Lord!

> *Revelations 3:20 says, "Here I am! Behold, I stand at the door and knock. If anyone hears my voice and opens the door, I will come in and eat with him, and he with me."*

Have you answered that knock? Have you given your life to Jesus? Have you told Him, "Thank you" for what He has done for you? Have you ever asked him to come in and take over? Here is where it all begins.

-8-
Life Is A Vapor

I thought I was indestructible in those early years and would live forever. I remember riding motorcycles, playing tackle football with older guys with no pads, making ramps out of anything I could find, and then jumping with my bike. The older I get, the more it's incredible how my thinking changes, and I sit here wondering who the older man I am looking at in the mirror is. How did I get to the age of fifty-six so fast? It seems like yesterday my girls were born, but they seemed to grow up overnight. I have so many fond memories of my girls growing up, and I could tell you story after story, and now they are both in their twenties. Where does the time go?

> *James 4:14 tells us, "Why, you do not even know what will happen tomorrow. What is your life? You are a vapor that appears for a little while and then vanishes."*

Talking about a rude awakening and seeing how fast life passes me is sobering. Life is like a vapor, and it only lasts for a very short time. We all like to believe we will all grow old and live to a good ripe age of 85, but let's not fool ourselves. If you drive a vehicle on any given day, that car from the other direction can cross that centerline and meet you head-on. Then your days would be cut short. I pray that doesn't happen to you, but it's possible. Because of that possibility, Jesus isn't just a part of my life; He is my life. Life is a vapor; it is here today and gone tomorrow. Because that is the truth, I want to make each day count. I want to make the most of my life here on earth. I want to ensure that people around me know how much I appreciate and love them. I know what is most important, or let me say it another way: Who is most important—the very One who holds my life in His hands. I seek the One who matters the most. I am devoted to Jesus.

I want to leave you with one more verse today, and I ask if you would pray through this scripture. Matthew 6:33-34 says,

> *"Seek first his kingdom and His righteousness, and all these things will be given to you as well. Therefore, do not worry about tomorrow; tomorrow will worry about itself. Each day has enough trouble of its own."*

I encourage you to live life like there is no tomorrow, put God first, and make the most of the opportunities in front of you today. Don't take your loved ones for granted; don't forget to tell them daily, "I love you." Tomorrow is just a bonus. God bless.

-9-
The Question Of Today

I have a question I want to ask you today, and I want to encourage you to take some time and think about it before you answer. I also ask that you spend some time praying through this question. Brace yourself and get ready; this is the question of the day: What is something you used to believe about yourself that Jesus came to cross out with the truth? There it is; what thoughts or images did that question trigger in your mind? For some, there was no doubt what Jesus set you free from; for others, it's more complicated. It may be multiple lies that Satan has tied you up with.

> *We all know what Jesus said in John 10:10, "The thief comes only to steal and kill and destroy; I have come that they may have life, and have it to the full."*

Satan is a liar, a thug, and a thief who wants to destroy your life. Not only does he want to kill you, but he also wants to take down those who love you the most. The enemy doesn't fight fair. The demonic will jump you in the dark alleys and trip you when you are unaware and least expect it. He is there to set that lie like a baited trap; then he will cover it and disguise it to catch you off guard. He wants to distract you from the truth, he wants you to spend time running lies through your mind, and he wants you to waste all your energy doing things that don't matter. Satan wants us to live in fear, he wants us to second-guess our salvation, and he wants us to keep our eyes on ourselves. What lies are you tracking today? Maybe Satan has told you, "God will never forgive you for that sin that haunts you till this day?" Have you heard that lie that says you are ugly, not loved, or hopelessly doomed to a place called hell? Maybe Satan has laid his trap for you and said, "Who needs God? You are your own god, or doesn't love and care for you?" What about this lie of Satan when he says, "Live your own life, do what feels good." Stop listening to the lies and turn to the Truth. It's a choice you have to make today.

When Satan comes to bully you, beat you up, and cover you with fear. Turn to truth, open up God's Word, and dive in. If you are in Christ, you are a child of God.

> *Romans 8:17 says, "Now if we are children, then we are heirs-heirs of God and co-heirs with Christ if indeed we share in his suffering in order that we may also share in his glory."*

You are a child of the Living God! You are an heir of the Lord. If you doubt your salvation or your eternal standing with Christ, read Romans 8:38-39. Which says this:

> *"For I am convinced that neither death nor life, neither angels nor demons, neither present nor future, nor any powers, neither height nor depth, nor anything else in all creation, will be able to separate us from the love of God that is in Christ Jesus."*

Nothing you can say or do can separate you from the love of God. He is a God of mercy, and He loves you very much. Don't live a life tied up with lies and deceit; cut yourself free with Truth and enjoy a new life in Jesus Christ.

Look what John 3:17 says,

Dennis L Taylor

"For God did not send his Son into the world to condemn the world, but to save the world through him."

Experience the freedom in Jesus Christ today.

-10-
Why Discipline?

I want to share some sound wisdom from scripture today. I know the word discipline brings back bad memories for some people. You can tell incredible stories that could make us all laugh, mainly when reflecting on your childhood.

> *Hebrews 12:7-11 says, "Endure hardship as discipline; God is treating you as sons. For what son is not disciplined by his father? If you are not disciplined, then you are illegitimate children and not true sons. Moreover, we have all had human fathers who disciplined us, and we respected them for it. How much more should we submit to the Father of our spirit and live? Our fathers disciplined us for a little while as they thought best, but God disciplines us for our good, that we may share in his holiness. No discipline seems pleasant at the time, but painful. Later on, however, it produces a harvest of righteousness and peace for those who have been trained by it."*

How many of us today can relate to the words of Paul in this text? The toughest football coach I ever had was Luther Welsh. He was a hardnose, old-school coach, and he demanded your respect. He worked you hard during practice and ensured you knew when you messed up or neglected your responsibility. If you didn't run a play right, you had to do it again until you executed it correctly.

The coach believed in wind sprints. After every practice, he would line the whole team on the goal line, place the whistle in his mouth, and blow it repeatedly; we would run until everyone was about to fall out. When I was an upcoming Sophomore quarterback, he expected me to know every play in the playbook. At times, I didn't think he liked me; he yelled at me more than anybody on the field. He scared me to death.

The following year, Coach Welsh left Dougherty High School for another school up North. He was the most demanding coach I ever played for, and it wasn't easy playing quarterback for him. I never thought I would say this, but I missed him that next year. Even though he made it hard on me, I learned something about him that I didn't appreciate until he was gone. He cared for me; he genuinely cared for me. He pushed me because he saw something I couldn't see in myself.

After my Sophomore year, I never saw Coach Welsh again, but at the end of my Senior year, I received a letter from Coach Welsh's College Alma Mater wanting me to come and play football for them. I found out later that he went out of his way to call the school to tell them about a kid in Southwest Georgia. He taught me hard work and discipline and went out of his way to show me how much he cared for me.

Don't shrug off God's discipline; it's the child he loves that he disciplines, the child he embraces and corrects. Think about it; only irresponsible parents leave children to fend for themselves. Would you prefer a reckless God?

I respected Coach Welsh for pushing and training me, so why not embrace God's training so we can really live? Knowing this, God is doing what is best for us and teaching us to live godly, holy lives.

Sometimes discipline isn't much fun, but in the long run, it makes you better. God sees something in you that is special, that you can't even see in yourself. Embrace the pain of growth and discipline. Life may be a struggle for you, but God is preparing and getting you ready, making you more like Christ.

-11-
Who Is Your Zacchaeus?

Luke 19:1-4: "Jesus entered Jericho and was passing through. A man was there by the name of Zacchaeus; he was a chief tax collector and was wealthy. He wanted to see who Jesus was, but being a short man, he could not because of the crowd. So he ran ahead and climbed a sycamore-fig tree to see him since Jesus was coming that way."

I remember growing up in church singing about Zacchaeus being a wee little man and climbing up in a sycamore tree to see Jesus. It was such a catchy little tune, but it didn't capture the crazy nature of the story. Zacchaeus wasn't just a short guy but a nasty guy. Yes, he was a thief, a crook, and a traitor. We should be singing this instead, "Zacchaeus was a total jerk, and a total jerk was he." We all know that Zacchaeus was a tax collector, a sellout, and a traitor. He betrayed his people for the Roman oppressors. Zacchaeus gained much wealth, extorting his fellow Jews, but all that wealth left him empty.

Look at Luke 19:5-8: "When Jesus reached the spot, he looked up and said to him, 'Zacchaeus, come down immediately. I must stay at your house today.' So he came down at once and welcomed him gladly. All the people saw this and began to mutter, 'He has gone to be the guest of 'sinners.' But Zacchaeus stood up and said to the Lord, 'Look, Lord! Here and now, I give half of my possessions to the poor, and if I have cheated anybody out of anything, I will pay back four times the amount."

Yes, Zacchaeus was an evil guy, but when he met Jesus face to face, his life changed instantly. He professed Jesus as Lord, and his heart changed. On the outside, Zacchaeus was calloused and cold, and it seemed like he had everything he ever wanted. On the inside, he was empty. I imagine Zacchaeus heard all the stories of Jesus' miracles and teachings, but he wanted to find out if it was true. I wonder how many people around us secretly desire to see Jesus. We say, "They will never go to church, or I know they don't want to hear about my Jesus." You know that person whom we say is a lost cause or they are too far gone to reach. That is your Zacchaeus. Luke 19:9-10, Jesus said:

"Today salvation has come to this house because this man too is the son of Abraham. For the Son of Man came to seek and to save what was lost."

There is no lost cause with Jesus, and nobody is beyond His reach. The challenge for today: Identify your Zacchaeus. Then, ask God to open a door of opportunity to share your story with them and tell them how Jesus has changed your life. I love that old saying that goes something like this: Before you talk to your friends about Jesus, speak to Jesus about your friends.

-12-
Cling

Have you ever gotten off a water ride at a theme park on a hot, sunny day? It cools you off, but your wet clothes cling to you until you dry out. It's not the best feeling in the world, but it helps you to understand the word *cling*. If that doesn't put a picture in your mind, think about the first time you rode a roller coaster. I held on tight to the bar in front of me. The word *cling* means to hold on tightly. I have found that every season of life that I've been through has required me to cling to my faith.

> *Deuteronomy 10:20: "You shall fear the Lord your God; you shall keep his commandments, listen to His voice, serve Him, and cling to Him."*

The instructions in this verse tell you what to do to cling to Him. We must fear and respect our Heavenly Father to realize how powerful He is. Know His commandments by daily reading and understanding His Word. Through His Word, the Holy Spirit can speak to you. Then, you can serve wholeheartedly, which glorifies Him. We must cling. The psalmist tells us how important it is to cling in Psalm 63:8:

> *"My soul clings to You, O my God, even as your right hand supports me."*

He loves us and wants to support us through every phase of life if we let Him.

Matthew 28:9" "They came to him, clasped his feet and worshiped him."

This verse describes when the women found Jesus alive in the empty tomb. They fell at Jesus' feet and worshiped him. To clasp means to hold or envelope someone or something. Cling and clasp mean the same thing. Be near Him, and don't let go. The toddlers are the smart ones. They know where their love, support, and protection come from.

The challenge for today: What are you holding on to today? Is it money, material goods, earthly relationships, jobs/positions, hobbies, or fun times? What are you waiting for? Fuel up through His word and prayer, know and fear Him, and serve others. Sit at His feet today. Clasp them tightly, and don't let go.

-13-
Trust Him

Raising kids is a never-ending task. It is a journey. Sometimes, it feels like you are riding a roller coaster. There are those super highs, and just around the corner, the bottom drops out. One thing is sure: parenting can be difficult, and you will make mistakes. But there is another truth: your kids will push you to your limits. They will do things that will drive you crazy and cause you to pull your hair out. Sometimes, I even questioned God why He would allow my children to act out in such a way. So many of us want to believe in God's presence and goodness, but sometimes we have many questions. We long to trust God, to feel His presence, to enjoy His peace, and to believe He is there for us. We want to know He hears us and will protect us and our families. But I know there are still some people who once believed that God took an active interest in their lives, but now they are not so sure.

Do you ever wonder where God was when your life fell apart, or how can God say He cared for me when my spouse passed away? How could God allow my child to go down the wrong path and run after the things of this world when I faithfully served Him? Why did I get laid off from my job? Does God care? Know this: you are not alone. Throughout the Bible, godly people questioned God's involvement in their lives and wondered where God was during a difficult time. We all have asked God about grief, temptation, and difficult times. We want to believe, but sometimes we will all struggle. Occasionally, we wonder if God sees our pain, and we will wonder if He cares.

If you are struggling, I pray you are willing to wrestle with God. He has never promised us that life will be easy or problem-free. To know God, you must wrestle through sorrow, doubt, unexplainable situations, and pain. If you are willing to wrestle with God and hold on to your faith, God will meet you in your confusion and distress. He will bring peace and comfort during your times of need. Trust Him.

> *Proverbs 3:5-6: "Trust in the Lord with all your heart and lean not on your own understanding; in all your ways acknowledge him, and he will make your path straight."*

Be willing to wrestle and trust Him because He cares for you.

The challenge for today: Memorize Proverbs 3:5-6. Hide this word in your heart and pull it out when hard times come. When difficult times come, take it in stride and bring it before the Lord before you can blow it out of proportion. It's okay to question God because we will not understand everything fully in this life. Be willing to wrestle with God in times of doubt, sorrow, and pain. But know this: He cares for you and loves you deeply. Trust Him today.

-14-
Wait

Habakkuk 3:2: "Then the Lord replied: Write down the revelation and make it plain on tablets so that a herald may run with it. For the revelation awaits an appointed time; it speaks of the end and will not prove false. Though it will linger, wait for it; it will certainly come and will not delay."

How many of us hate to wait? What about those long lines in Saxby's drive-through? It takes forever to get a big Zax Snack. Whatever happened to fast food? One of the most frustrating things in life is the big city traffic. Can I get an Amen? O, how we hate to see those brake lights on a crowded eight-lane highway. Growing up, one of the hardest things to do was wait for Christmas because you were so excited to play with all your new toys. Christmas could not come soon enough. An old saying goes like this: "God is rarely early, never late, and always right on time." You see, God has a plan, and it will happen on His timetable, whether we like it or not. Sometimes, all we can do is wait.

When God promises you something, it will come to pass. But it will be in His timing. Part of every believer's faith involves waiting on God and His promises to be fulfilled. In Exodus chapter three, Moses was promised that God would use him to deliver His people from slavery and make Israel a great nation. Then Moses went on a forty-year road trip. What about a guy named Joseph? In Genesis chapter 37, that same God promised to be a great leader and would rule over his brothers. What happened to Joseph? His brothers threw him in a pit and sold him into slavery, where his master's wife falsely accused him. Then, he was thrown in jail, and he waited. Thirteen years went by before God fulfilled His promise. What are you waiting on? But the more important question is this: what are you doing while you wait?

> *Colossians 3:17: "And whatever you do, whether in word or deed, do it all in the name of the Lord Jesus, giving thanks to God the Father through him."*

Even when you don't understand what God is up to, continue to serve Him. It's not easy, but that is where faith comes in.

The challenge for today: Answer this question: what are you waiting on? While you wait, stay focused on your relationship with Jesus Christ and serve him faithfully.

-15-
Remember

Here is the truth today. The older you get, the harder it is to remember. Don't you hate it when it comes time to change your passwords to all the different programs and functions on your computer? Just when you are getting used to plugging in that password, it is time to change it again. My wife and I have to keep a little black book in our kitchen drawer to keep up with all our passwords. It's almost an impossible task. What about those faces from the past that you have not seen in a while? You recognize the faces, but you cannot remember their names. We remember what matters most to us because we replay it often in our memories. For example, I grew up watching a sitcom called The Brady Bunch. I would watch it daily and repeatedly sing along to the beginning song. To this day, some forty years later, I can still remember every word of that song. I love going back in time and remembering those special times in my childhood and years past. I have had so much fun playing sports, marrying my childhood sweetheart, having kids, and living life.

But we all know that life can also be challenging. There will be valleys that we will pass through, and we will get knocked down. If you are traveling in a valley today and going through a tough time, the best way to climb out is to remember what God has done for you in the past. In the first chapter of Habakkuk, the prophet asks God some difficult questions, and he wants some answers. But in Habakkuk 3:2 Habakkuk was saying:

"I know what kind of God you are. I have seen your power. I have experienced your presence. Please do it again."

Today, recall how faithful God has been to you in your past. I remember playing with my girls in the pool when they were little. I can recall the sounds, the laughing, and the splashes in the pool. I remember throwing them high in the air and how they landed in the water. They responded, "Do it again, Daddy, do it again!" When you are facing hard times, remember how faithful God has been to you in the past. Return to who you know God is. Don't be scared to ask Him to do it again. He is faithful, and He cares for you.

The challenge for today: The God of the mountains is also the God of the valleys. He will never leave us or forsake us. Dare to believe what He has done in the past. He will do it again. Fuel up, stay positive, and trust in His faithfulness.

-16-
Open Your Eyes

Romans 3:23: "All have sinned and come short of the glory of God."

How many times have we read this verse? I have used this verse hundreds of times when I have shared my faith. Yes, we all have fallen short and messed up, and none of us are perfect. There is not a single person who would argue that point. But we all have allowed our past to weigh us down and take us out. The Devil loves to use our past failures and slip-ups to discourage us, disqualify us, and cause us to sit on the sidelines of life. He loves to overwhelm us with negativity and despair. The enemy loves it when we don't lean into God's promises and when we replay our sins repeatedly in our minds. He also loves it when we disqualify ourselves from serving God and not being obedient to what God has called us to do. Have we allowed guilt, lies, and past regrets to kill our passion for the things of God? Have we become distracted from the things that matter? There comes a time when we have to say, "Enough is enough." It is time to move past the lies. It is time to move past the guilt. It is time to receive His grace and move forward with what God has called us to be in Christ Jesus.

Here is another familiar scripture that needs to ring out in ears today.

Romans 6:23: "For the wages of sin is death, but the gift of God is eternal life in Christ Jesus."

We deserve death, discouragement, and destruction. We deserve to carry that load of guilt that weighs us down. But thank God, Jesus paid the price for our freedom and deliverance from that bondage. We no longer have to live in failure and pain. We have been set free because of the blood of Jesus. Can we thank God for His mercy and grace? God has made forgiveness available to all who believe in Jesus. Open your eyes to the truth God has for you, and don't believe the lies the devil wants to deceive you. Use your yesterday to spread hope, encouragement, and love. Don't see your past failures and mess-ups as a disqualifier but as a tool that God can use to encourage others. Don't see your past weaknesses as a waste but as fertilizer to grow God's love in others. What the Devil meant for harm, God will use for His glory.

The challenge for Today: Confess your sins to the Lord, and get your heart right with Him. Receive His grace and mercy, and let go of the guilt and heaviness you have been carrying for so long. Begin to walk in freedom and open your eyes to the opportunities God places before you. Take time to thank Him for His love and His willingness to give us Jesus.

-17-
Keep Love at the Front of the Line

Philippians 2:3-5: "Do nothing from selfish ambition or conceit, but in humility count others more significant than yourselves. Let each of you look not only to his own interests but also to the interests of others. Have this mind among yourselves, which is yours in Christ Jesus."

I believe in hard work, which my dad taught me early in life. I used to watch him build an addition to our house all by himself. He was very determined and had the attitude that nothing would stop him from completing a project. He had my brother and me out early on Saturday to cut our acre lot with a single push mower; without a doubt, he taught us what it meant to have a strong work ethic. From that day on, I adopted an attitude that no one was going to outwork me, and I wanted to be the best at whatever I attempted to pursue in life, whether it was work, ministry, or just being a dad.

We must be careful regarding ministry and our relationship with Jesus. I still believe that working hard is very important, but if we aren't focused on loving Jesus, forcing that work ethic into a performance-based relationship with Christ can be easy. How easy is it to fall into that snare of earning our salvation or trying to earn the respect of other church members? It is so easy to lose sight of why you started serving in the first place. Whenever we serve, whether praying, ushering, taking up the offering, teaching, or singing a solo in the Christmas musical, let it be out of gratitude for what Jesus Christ has done for us. As we serve, we keep love at the front of the line regarding our motivation and passion for helping others.

> *Second Corinthians 5:14: "It is Christ's love that fuels our passions and motivates us because we are absolutely convinced that he has given his life for all of us. This means all died with him."*

The challenge for today is to examine your motivation for serving others. Be willing to ask yourself hard questions regarding your reason for working in the Church. Let's get back to loving people just like Jesus. Please don't fall for a performance-based relationship because it will leave you empty and worn out. Make sure you take in His love daily and do not give away more than you receive. What is at the front of your line? I pray that it is love.

Dennis L Taylor

-18-
The Fear of Man

Paul was writing to the Church of Galatia, a Church that he had planted, which is located in the center of what is now known as Asia Minor. Many Jews lived in this area at the time. The Galatians were noted for fickleness and love for new and curious things. The Galatian Church was facing a double threat that involved purity of doctrine and purity of conduct. They insisted that, while salvation was of Christ, works were also necessary for salvation. Because of their thought process, Paul shared a critical message with the Church that we need to hear today.

> Galatians 1:10: "Am I now trying to win the approval of men, or of God? Or am I trying to please men? If I were still trying to please men, I would not be a servant of Christ."

Our society is based on likes and followers. It is sad to say, but that is the truth. Have you ever found yourself trying to defend who you are? Do you live in fear of what people think of you? When you are living in a spirit of fear, worrying every second about what people say about you or so concerned about how you look, you are living in a cage. You are placing yourself in a self-contained prison when you could be walking in freedom. People-pleasing is a dangerous trap to fall into. It can be a slippery slope that leads you to a deep hole, and you can struggle for years trying to escape it. It will cost you time, energy, and a lot of effort. Do you fight

38

to get recognition? Are you striving to prove yourself and your worth to other people? This fear can paralyze you, which is not how God asked you to live.

> First John 4:18: "There is no fear in love. But perfect love drives out fear, because fear has to do with punishment. The one who fears is not made perfect in love."

I want to challenge you not to operate out of a spirit of fear and stop wasting so much energy trying to please everyone. That can be exhausting; believe me, I know. Let everything you do come from love, and try your best to please your Heavenly Father. Look for the approval of One. Think about it: Jesus himself was a peacemaker, not a peacekeeper. He said and did what was good, different from what was popular that day. Ask God for strength to overcome this worry and fear and walk in complete freedom. Operate out of love.

-19-
His Love

First John 4:7-10: "Dear friends, let us love one another, for love comes from God. Everyone who loves has been born of God and knows God. Whoever does not love does not know God, because God is love. This is how God showed his love among us: He sent his one and only Son into the world that we might live through him. This is love: not that we loved God, but that he loved us and sent his Son as an atoning sacrifice for our sins."

That is a powerful message that the Church needs to hear. Listen, our job as believers in Jesus Christ isn't to make people love Jesus but to love one another through the good and the bad and to tell the world about God's amazing love. This world is looking for a source of happiness and peace, and they are coming up short. You can have all this world has to offer and still not be happy or content. We must share the Gospel message with those without Jesus and tell them how much God loves them. Let them know what God gave up for them to experience true life and joy. He gave up His only Son to die on an old, rugged cross. Jesus suffered, bled, and died so we could have an authentic life. Can the world see the love of God in your life and in how you treat others? Do they notice a difference between walking in the room and how you carry yourself?

First John 4:11-12: "Dear friends, since God so loved us, we should also love one another. No one has ever seen God; but if we love one another, God lives in us, and his love is made complete in us."

When you experience the love of God, it will change your viewpoint. It will change your dreams, passions, and your outlook on life. It will also change how you see people around you and respond to challenging situations. His love, coupled with obedience, can be the catalyst that moves God to respond to your prayers powerfully, and it is in that place you will find peace and freedom. Love one another, and let the glory of God shine through you. Loving people who hurt will shut down the enemy's plans and his ability to create division. When we love others the same way God loves us, it drives Satan crazy.

The challenge for today: Take a few minutes to thank God for His amazing love. Then, ask the Lord, "Whom do I need to share His love with today?" If someone is hard to love, ask God for strength and wisdom. Make sure you follow through with what He is showing you.

-20-
Don't Give Up

Seven weeks ago, I started working out again after doing nothing to take care of my physical body. Trying to get up early and commit to attending the gym at 5:30 a.m. was tough. Thank goodness I had some accountabilities put in place to hold my feet to the fire. It has been a while since I had this much physical activity. Since I am a sports and recreational Pastor, I play basketball with a bunch of guys on Sunday, and we also just started a softball league. For the first time, I had to catch my breath after taking thirty swings during batting practice.

I used to pride myself in being a pretty good athlete, but at 56, many of my skills and abilities left the room. What I took for granted back in the day, like running fast, jumping high, or catching six-fly ball on the run, is not so easy anymore. I would lie if I told you I felt good and excited about being physically active again. But the truth is, my body hurts, and I am always tired. Some days, it is hard to sit down and get back up. It is sad, but I am sharing the truth with you. My body screams at me, "What are you doing? Are you trying to take me out?" It would be so easy to give up. It would be much easier to sleep in than go to the gym. I could organize the basketball and softball league; then, I wouldn't be so sore and constantly hurt.

Have you ever asked yourself this question: How did I get here? How did I get so out of shape so fast? Personal fitness took a back seat, and other things became more critical for me. With everything going on as a dad, husband, ministry, and work, I pushed personal fitness aside and neglected what was once so important to me.

What about your relationship with God? Maybe there was a time when God held first place in your heart, and He was your number one priority. Over time, life happens, and other things become more important to you, and God takes that back seat in your life when He should be driving. You tried to rekindle that fire and passion you once had, but it takes too much effort, and I will have to drop other things that I love to do. Maybe you are beat up and worn out by the ministry, or someone hurt your feelings, so you just quit and give up on God because that is the easiest thing to do. Have you ever asked yourself this question regarding your relationship with God: How did I get here?

Galatians 6:9: "Let us not become weary in doing good, for at the proper time we will reap a harvest if we do not give up."

The challenge for today: You may be tired, beat up, and spiritually sore, but hang in there. Don't give up or roll over on God. I encourage you to press forward, keep your eyes on Christ, and ensure accountability partners are in place. Expect difficult situations and challenging people to come your way, but keep Christ in the first chair of your life. There will be resistance, but resistance makes you stronger. Rekindle that passion that you once had for Jesus and push through the spiritual soreness.

-21-
Dare To Dream

I love to get up early in the morning, especially on Saturdays. I let my wife sleep, and I have hours to spend with the Lord, soaking in His presence and reflecting on the week. I don't want to come across as super spiritual; it's more of recharging and getting my mind back in proper perspective. It is easy to lose focus and get off track of what God calls me to do and be. This is a time when I don't have to be in a hurry, and I don't have to rush away somewhere. In the stillness of this quiet place, God challenges me to dream. In the quietness of the moment, in the very presence of God, the routine of my week fades away. The dullness of day is brought to light. Then the Lord inspires me, words to speak encouragement, and He fills my spiritual cup to overflowing. "Thank you, Lord Jesus." My time of reflection becomes a time of excitement, passion, and dreaming.

What has God placed in your heart? It may be passing thoughts, daydreams, flashes of pictures, or particular scriptures that always seem to pop up. What one desire continually makes your heart race or puts you on the edge of your seat? It is there for a reason. God has a plan and purpose for it, and He is always trying to lead you to your God-dream. How many of us have a passion or a dream but never dare to go after it? We find ourselves running away in fear and shrinking back to mundane living. Then we become satisfied with the norm, content with the same old, and never experience the thrill of life in Christ.

Genesis 37:5-8: "Joseph had a dream, and when he told it to his brothers, they hated him all the more. He said to them, 'Listen to this dream I had: We were binding sheaves of grain out in the fields when suddenly my sheaf rose and stood upright, while your sheaves gathered mine and bowed down to it.' His brothers said to him, "Do you intend to reign over us? Will you actually rule us?' And they hated him all the more because of his dream and what he had said."

I don't want to write a feel-good devotional without telling you the truth. Having a God-dream is great, but it will not always be the easiest path. If you have the guts to follow your passion and your dreams, there will be obstacles to overcome and difficulties to face. Get ready for the trying times and the leaps of faith you must take to continue the journey. Chasing God-dreams will not be easy, but it will be worth it. Joseph faced many difficult situations, trials, and temptations along the way, but he didn't falter or shrink back from the dream that God placed in him. He didn't stop dreaming because it got hard or people didn't believe in him. Because of his unwavering faith, he saved his family and the nation of Israel.

The challenge for today: Dare to dream. Set aside time to get alone with God, and don't be in a hurry to run away. Rest in Him, turn your focus away from worldly concerns, and turn your spiritual eyes to the God of the universe. Write down what the Lord shares with you, and don't be surprised if what He tells you makes you feel very uncomfortable. Run the race of faith and carry the God dream with you. It may get complicated, but the finish line has a way of making it all worth it. What is God calling you to do? Pursue it, run after it, and keep your focus on Him.

-22-
Receive His Instructions

There are two things that God is sliding in front of me these days. First, He is convicting me of my unbelief. I pray these enormous prayers, and as soon as they leave my lips, I doubt His power and authority. One would think I would be more confident in a God who has been so faithful to me. He has never failed me, and He shows me His favor daily. "Lord, forgive me for my unbelief." The second thing God is showing me every day is to encourage others continuously. This is my purpose and calling for the last third of my life. Every morning, I pray that the Lord will provide opportunities to encourage others and push them closer to Christ.

> *Hebrews 3:12-15: "See to it, brothers, that none of you has a sinful, unbelieving heart that turns away from the living God. But encourage one another daily, as long as it is called Today, so that none of you may be hardened by sin's deceitfulness. We have come to share in Christ if we hold firmly till the end the confidence we had at first. As has just been said: 'Today, if you hear his voice, do not harden your hearts as you did in the day of rebellion.'"*

The generation that came out of Egypt did not enter the Promised Land because of their unbelief. The Lord performed miracle after miracle, providing them daily with food and water. But all they could do was grumble and complain. The Lord allowed them to come to a new level of intimacy with Him, but they chose to stay at a distance and do their own thing, their way. Because of their unbelief, the Children of Israel wandered in the desert for forty years. Can you relate to the Children of Israel? He gave them a promise, but they doubted His power and authority, so they missed out on God's best.

I want you to experience God's best today. I encourage you to hear the voice of God, write down His promises, and stand on them. Don't stumble in doubt, fear, or fall away because of delays and not understanding God's timing. Nobody has ever said this life would be easy, but we must continue to press forward and trust in a God in complete control. I want to wrap this up with words from Joshua 1:6-8.

> *"Be strong and courageous, because you will lead these people to inherit the land I swore to their forefathers to give them. Be strong and very courageous. Be careful to obey all the laws my servant Moses gave you; do not turn from it to the right or the left so that you may be successful wherever you go. Do not let this Book of the Law depart from your mouth; meditate on it day and night to be careful to do everything written in it. Then you will be prosperous."*

The challenge for today: Stand firm in what God has told you. Be strong and courageous. As you walk out your faith daily, don't forget to encourage others because it pleases the Lord.

-23-
Unforgettable Walks

My wife and I take our dog, Luca, on a daily walk around our neighborhood. It gives us a chance to say hello to the neighbors and time for Laura and me to catch up on each other's workday. Plus, it allows Luca to leave the house and release some energy. He loves to look for squirrels and rabbits. It seemed to be her favorite time of day, and he knew when it was time to go on his walk. The Bible has a list of unforgettable walks. Take a look at several walks that we can read about in God's Word:

1. Abraham's walk with his son Isaac on the road to Moriah.
2. Moses and the Israelites walked through the Red Sea.
3. Joshua's victorious walk around Jericho.
4. Paul's life-changing walk on Damascus Road.
5. Jesus' walk up Golgotha Hill.

But perhaps the most unforgettable walk was taken by Peter when he got out of the boat and walked to Jesus on the water. Peter's walk represents an invitation to everyone who wants to step out on faith and experience more of the power of God. There is a pattern in scripture of what happens when people are willing to be used by God.

- **There is always a call. God loves to use ordinary people to do extraordinary things.**

- **There is always fear. From Moses to us today. He has a way of calling us out of our comfort zone and forcing us to take giant steps of faith.**
- **There will be reassurance. God promises us that He will never leave us or forsake us.**
- **There is always a decision. Will we say yes or no?**
- **There is always a changed life.**

Matthew 14:25-30: "During the fourth watch of the night Jesus went out to them, walking on the lake. When the disciples saw him walking on the lake, they were terrified. 'It's a ghost,' they said and cried out in fear. But Jesus immediately said to them: 'Take courage! It is I. Don't be afraid. 'Lord, if it's you,' Peter replied, "tell me to come to you on the water.' 'Come,' he said. Then Peter got out of the boat, walked on the water, and came towards Jesus. But when he saw the winds, he was afraid and, beginning to sink, cried out, 'Lord save me!'"

Jesus speaks those exact words to us daily. "Come to Me." He is calling us out of our boat of comfort and asking us to be willing to do something different. Get ready to throw your feet over the side of the boat and dangle them in the water. When he calls you to something new and different, keep your eyes on Him.

-24-
Step Out

I remember the first time I taught a lesson in front of a group. I was so nervous, and I was shaking. I knew the Lord wanted me to do this, but speaking in front of people was my greatest fear. I had to step my game up, step out on faith, and trust Him with the results. What has God asked you to do over the years that has caused you great stress? Has He asked you to get out of your boat of comfort or routine? Answering God's call can be exciting, scary, and overwhelming all at the same time. One minute, you are pumped and filled with joy. You are overcome with fear the next minute and wonder what I have done. What does it take to step out on faith? What does it take to do what God has called you to do?

1. Recognize God's Presence.

Jesus wanted to be alone with His disciples, so He told them to get in the boat and go ahead of Him while He dismissed the crowd. Jesus went to pray, and the disciples began to row. As they rowed, a storm rolled in, the wind started to blow, and the waves began slamming against the boat. If that wasn't enough, one of the disciples noticed a shadow moving towards them on the water. The disciples were convinced that it was a ghost. They were terrified, scared, and afraid. But it was Jesus walking on water. Jesus was revealing his divine presence and power. Twelve disciples sat in the boat, but only one walked on water. Peter recognized that Jesus was present even in the most unlikely place.

2. Discern between faith and foolishness.

Matthew 14:28-29: "Lord, if it's you,' Peter replied, 'tell me to come to you on the water.' 'Come,' he said." Why didn't Peter plunge right into the water? This isn't a story about risk; it's a story of obedience. We must discern between an authentic call from God or a foolish impulse on our part. Courage is not enough; it must be accompanied by wisdom and discernment. That means before Peter got out of the boat, he better make sure Jesus thought it was a good idea.

3. Be willing to step away from comfort.

Some of the disciples were seasoned fishermen. They have grown up in a boat. But there was something different about this storm. The boat represented safety, security, and comfort. You must get out of the boat to walk on the water. You are made for something more than merely avoiding failure. We are called to leave comfort and routine; we must abandon selfishness and pride. Your boat is whatever you are tempted to put your trust in, especially when life gets rough. Don't shrink back. Place your trust in Jesus.

4. Expect Problems.

Peter goes to the side of the boat. The other disciples were watching closely. They had heard Peter run his mouth before and wondered how far he would take it this time. Can you see Peter dipping his toe in the water and grabbing the side of that boat? Peter let go of the boat and started walking toward Jesus. Then he took his eyes off Jesus, and the wind and the wave caught his attention. Then he began to sink. Reality set in. Trouble has a way of catching us by surprise.

There is danger in getting out of the boat. But there is also danger in never leaving the boat. Jesus is inviting you to an adventure of a lifetime. Don't live a life trapped in fear. Choose to live a life of faith.

-25-
Choose To Grow

Following Jesus is choosing to grow and being willing to place yourself in situations where fear constantly jumps in your face. When Peter exited the boat and faced the storm, he walked on water. Then his eyes drifted; he saw the winds and became afraid. Jesus said, "Don't be afraid." Do you think that was the last time in Peter's life he had to face fear? Certainly not. Fear will never go away as long as we continue to grow in Christ. A decision to grow always involves a choice between risk and comfort.

As a result of seeing the wind and being overcome with fear, Peter begins to sink. So the question is, did Peter fail? That is a tricky question to answer, but here is my answer. There were eleven bigger failures still sitting in the boat. Yes, Peter faced scrutiny from his friend group, but only Peter knew the glory of walking on water. Only Peter knew the glory of being helped out of the water by Jesus. Peter's willingness to risk failure enabled him to grow in such a way that the other eleven never could understand.

> *Matthew 14:31: "Immediately Jesus reached out his hand and caught him. 'You of little faith,' he said, 'why did you doubt?'"*

We all can relate to this verse. How many times have we started so well? We are full of faith, and our eyes are on Jesus. Things are going so well, and everything is running smoothly. Then, the storms of this life grab our attention, we become distracted, and we begin to sink into selfishness and sin. There will be times when we will fall flat on our faces. There will be times when we become overwhelmed with discouragement and doubt. Failure doesn't shape us, but how we respond to that failure grows us. You see, it was Peter's willingness to risk failure that helped him to grow. I don't mind taking risks. It's exciting not knowing what is going to happen. But I struggle with waiting on the Lord, especially during the storms of life.

> *Matthew 14:25 says, "During the fourth watch of the night, Jesus went out to them, walking on the lake."*

The disciples had to wait in the storm until the fourth watch of the night. Why didn't Jesus come in the first watch of the night? Why couldn't Jesus have made the wind die down before Peter got out of the boat? We may never know those answers until we see Jesus face to face. Waiting on the Lord is the hardest part of trusting Him fully. It's about being willing to place ourselves in the hands of the Lord and say, "Take over, Lord; I am yours." He calls us to total dependence and complete surrender. When we finally give Him our all, don't get in a hurry to arrive at our destination. It will take some rowing, much faith, and a willingness to wait on Him. He will most likely wait to reveal His purpose to us in the fourth watch of the night. But it will be worth the wait.

-26-
Three Encouragements

There is so much negativity in our world today. Turn on the news, and it will leave you depressed and unsettled. The pressures of life tend to build over time, like paying the bills, demands at work, and raising kids. I don't want to disappoint you, but I want to give you encouragement and hope. Here are three things that will help you along your journey and encourage you along the way.

- **First, guard against distractions.**

We know how the story ends; Jesus Christ is coming again. We are on the winning team! Jesus has overcome the grave, sin, and death. Can I get an Amen? But Satan isn't going down without a fight. He has come to steal, kill, and destroy. He loves to use distractions to take you and your family out. Distractions pull your focus off Christ and place it on something else. If the devil can't make you bad, he will make you busy. He will distract you in so many ways. He will get you so busy thinking about your hobby that you have no time for God's Word. Shut the door of distractions. Slow down, refocus, and return to your first love.

- **Second, be bold and full of courage.**

When God calls you to a task, He will push you out of your comfort zone. We all know that from experience. When this happens, know that God is not punishing you but preparing you. Moses felt overwhelmed when God told him to approach Pharaoh. Gideon felt the pressure when God took his army of 32,000 and shrank it to 300 men. Even Jesus experienced the agony of dying on an old, rugged cross. Situations like this will require boldness and total dependence on God. Stand firm and be willing to face difficult obstacles head-on. Don't hesitate to lean on the God of the universe.

- **Third, make it all about Jesus.**

Have you ever noticed how easy it is to get off track? It happens, even when it comes to church. Attending church can quickly become about power, control, position, and pride. It shouldn't be about you and your opinion. I know this sounds so religious, but it is true. It needs to be all about Jesus. The very Son of God. The Savior of my soul. The very One who left the splendor of heaven to save each one of us by shedding His precious blood on a cross.

> Hebrews 3:1 says, "Holy brothers, who share in the heavenly calling, fix your thoughts on Jesus, the apostle and high priest whom we confess.

Take away: I encourage you to guard against distractions, be bold and courageous, and make it all about Jesus. Stay focused on what is essential and what lasts forever. Dig into God's Word and gain strength and wisdom. Don't waver in the things of this world, but place your trust in the God of the universe. Make sure that Jesus is your number one focus, and everything else will fall into place.

-27-
Build Up

If you want to build on the foundation of Jesus Christ, you must start with time alone with God. Some call this their quiet time. As believers in Christ, we need time to soak in the presence of God. I love to say it like this: grilled chicken is good, but when you marinate it in sauce, chicken goes to the next level. When we commit to soaking or marinade in the very presence of God, he will take us to another level of living. But it starts with a commitment.

First, set aside time every day to meet with the Lord. Block that time out every day. This is where you make your relationship with God a priority.

Psalm 143:8 says, "Let the morning bring me word of unfailing love, for I have put my trust in you. Show me the way I should go, for you I lift up my soul."

I strongly advocate meeting with God first thing in the morning. I want to get my marching orders and the directions I will need for the day. There are days when I will need all the wisdom and encouragement I can get. Jesus himself took time in the morning to spend with his Father.

Mark 1:35 says, "Very early in the morning, while it was still dark, Jesus got up, left the house, and went off to a solitary place, where he prayed."

Don't forget that Jesus is our greatest example. Yes, He is the total package. If our Lord needed His time alone with God, how much more do we need this time? If the Devil can't make you bad, he will make you busy. Imagine you were on a trip; you have been driving for some time and are rushing to reach your destination. You are running low on gas, and you need to stop to refuel. You find a gas station, but you have so much going on, and you are running a little late. A man is attending the pumps and waiting for you to stop to fill up your car's gas tank. You are in such a hurry that you don't have time to stop. So, you keep riding around the gas pumps and tell the attendant to give you twenty dollars' worth of gas. In the gas attendant's frustration, he does the best possible job to hit your gas tank. But most of the gas ended up on the ground. Then you pull off, and you take off on your journey. I know that sounds crazy and probably will never happen in real life, but that is what is happening spiritually in many of our lives. We stay so busy, running from one appointment to another. Never slowing down, and we are running on empty. Sooner or later, it will leave you physically, mentally, and emotionally beside the road.

Here is a simple truth that we all need to hear. Slow down! Learn how to enjoy your time alone with God. Take time to soak in His presence and receive from your Heavenly Father. Get away from all the distractions of life. Get away from cell phones, emails, and all electronics. Find a quiet place and commit to meeting with Him every day. You may be asking why you are stressing the importance of meeting with God. Why is this time so important? Because it is important to Him, and He created us for fellowship.

-28-
Take A Look

First Thessalonians 5:17-18 says, "Pray continually; give thanks in all circumstances, for this is God's will for you in Christ Jesus."

Pray continually; that means talking and listening to the Father throughout your day and being thankful for all the blessings of life. God is good, and He is good all the time. Prayer can change your world, and it can even change your attitude about life. If you are a worrier, start praying. If you are depressed and overwhelmed, pray. Worrying is taking responsibility for something God never intended for us to handle. In whom or what do we put our trust? I'm giving you three things that will help you to stay focused on the main thing.

1. **Make deliberate choices and efforts to set your mind on Christ.**

    Colossians 3:1, "Since then, you have been raised with Christ, set your hearts on things above, where Christ is seated at the right hand of God.

2. **Make a deliberate choice to exercise your mind on Christ. In other words, practice His presence.
    Keep a continuous conversation going with your Heavenly Father.**

3. **Carry this exercise of setting your mind on God into every area of life. It doesn't matter how small or how big the situation is.**

I encourage you to pray specifically. You will see and experience the very power of God. I also want to take another step forward and encourage you to journal. Begin to write down your prayers and what God is showing you. Your prayer life will come alive. God is calling His Church to pray and to pray with actions.

-29-
What?

I have a couple of questions I want to ask you today. They are not hard questions to answer, but be honest with yourself and answer them as honestly as possible.

- **What is your mind full of right now?**
- **What are you thinking about?**
- **Are you in a constant state of fear and constantly worried about tomorrow?**
- **How will you pay all your bills or make it to the next paycheck?**
- **Is your heart filled with anxiety?**
- **Are you dreading the day and wishing you could stay in bed?**
- **Are you overwhelmed with the death of a loved one or a broken relationship?**
- **Is your marriage in trouble, and you don't know what to do to repair it?**
- **Do you always feel drained, and you can never get enough rest?**
- **Are your kids out of control, and are you ready to give up?**
- **Have you ever felt like you have been pushed into a corner and don't have the strength to fight back?**

All of us, at some time or another, have felt discouraged, defeated, and overwhelmed. You may be walking in a tough season of life, and you feel like God is a thousand miles away. Nothing seems to go your way, and you need more desire to ask for help. The joy you once had for life is gone, and negative thoughts flood your mind constantly. You feel beat up, forgotten, and tired. If this is you, I want to pour God's Word of encouragement over you and let you know that you are not alone and that God is enough.

> *Isaiah 43:1-3: "But now, this is what the Lord says-he who created you, O Jacob, he who formed you, O Israel: 'Fear not, for I have redeemed you; I have summoned you by name; you are mine. When you pass through the waters, I will be with you, and when you pass through the rivers, they will not sweep over you. When you walk through the fire, you will not be burned; the flames will not set you ablaze. For I am the Lord, your God, the Holy One of Israel, your Savior.'"*

Fear not; if you are a child of God, you have been redeemed. In other words, you have been made right in the eyes of God because of the Blood of Jesus. You have been forgiven, and the very Creator of heaven and earth loves you. Yes, you may be going through a difficult time, and things may seem like they are falling apart, but hang in there! Don't give up. Don't roll over, and certainly don't wave the white flag to the enemy who is out to destroy you. Jesus is right by your side, holding your hand, drying your tears, and giving you a shoulder to cry on. Lean on Him for strength and comfort. Push aside pride today, cry to God, and say, "I need you!"

First Peter 5:6-7: "Humble yourselves, therefore, under God's mighty hand, that he may lift you in due time. Cast all your anxiety on him because he cares for you."

The challenge for Today: Stop listening to the lies of Satan. Fill your mind with truth, and remind yourself daily that He is with you every step of the way. He doesn't leave your side and has given you everything you need to win the battle and climb any difficult mountain. He is more than enough! Cast your cares and worries at the feet of Jesus. Then leave them there and continue to walk out your faith journey. Remind yourself that you are on the winning team. You are a Warrior of Christ, and God loves you.

-30-
Unclog The Lines

How does the presence and power of the Holy Spirit become a reality in our lives? This is the million-dollar question in the Church today. The New Testament teaching on being filled with the Holy Spirit can be wrapped up in three terms: Understanding, Submission, and Walking by Faith.

The first step in being filled with the Spirit is understanding. We must know that God has given us His Holy Spirit, and He dwells within us. We must also understand that God commands us to be filled with the Spirit. That means it is His will for us to be filled. He wants us to live a life controlled and guided by the Holy Spirit.

Luke 11:13 says, "If you then, being evil, know how to give good gifts to your children, how much more shall the Heavenly Father give the Holy Spirit to those who ask Him?"

This leads me to ask a question. What blocks the work of the Holy Spirit in our lives? It is a sin. Before we are filled with the Holy Spirit, we must deal honestly and entirely with every known sin in our hearts. This may be more challenging than you thought. Yes, it can be painful, but it is necessary to take the next step. There will be no filling of the Holy Spirit apart from cleansing from sin. Identify your sins and acknowledge them to the Father.

I love my old coffee pot; it has produced some of the best coffee in the world. But I notice it takes longer and longer to brew every couple of months. When that happens, I know that calcium buildup is beginning to block the flow of that black java. So, I find a jar of vinegar, pour it into my coffee maker, and hit the brew button. Then I let it run through the whole process, and the vinegar acts as a cleaning agent and clears out any blockage that will stop the flow of the black gold.

In the same way, our lives need that chemical provided by the blood of Christ to unclog the pipes of our hearts. Sin clogs our hearts and stops the flow of the Holy Spirit in our lives. The blood of Jesus is the great cleanser when applied by repentance and faith.

> *First John 1:7-9: "But if we walk in the light, as he is in the light, we have fellowship with one another, and the blood of Jesus, his Son, purifies us from all sin. If we claim to be without sin, we deceive ourselves and the truth is not in us. If we confess our sins, he is faithful and just and will forgive us our sins and purify us from all unrighteousness."*

The challenge for Today: Take time to identify what is blocking the flow of the Holy Spirit in your life. Then confess that to the Lord, tell Him you are sorry, and ask Him to cleanse you from all your unrighteousness. Let Him move freely in your life and remove all that sin build up so the Holy Spirit can flow through you and produce great joy and purpose. Give the Lord some praise for the life-cleansing blood of Jesus.

-31-
Understanding

Before a person comes to Christ, there is only one force at work in us-the old carnal nature. But thank God, the Holy Spirit dwells within us when we accept Christ. Now, there are two natures at work in our lives. Which of the two natures will rule over your actions? Unless the Holy Spirit controls your life, we will be dominated by our old nature. The work of the Holy Spirit will be blocked.

We must deal with the sin that controls our lives. Pride is often the root of all our sins and why we struggle so much with our relationship with God. Sin has a way of blinding us, distorting our view from the truth, and we can't see how much it has invaded every area of our lives. We often want what Jesus has for us, but we want to cling to our sins even more. There may be an issue with jealousy, unclean thoughts, or unforgiveness towards a brother or sister in Christ. These heart issues and worldly filth can pile up overnight if we don't keep our eyes open and guard our hearts.

That is why daily confession is so important. We need that restored fellowship with the Father. Sin will always be a continual issue, and it will be marked by defeat and discouragement as long as we keep "self" at the center of our lives. It blows me away how many Christians never really face this issue of Christ's Lordship. He calls us to renounce our plans and dreams and place Him above everything else. He asks us to step off the throne of our lives and allow Him to step in and sit on the throne of our hearts.

Luke 9:23-24: "Then he said to them all: 'If anyone would come after me, he must deny himself and take up his cross daily and follow me. For whoever wants to save his life will lose it, but whoever loses his life for me will save it.'"

Second Corinthians 5:15 says, "And he died for all, that those who live should no longer live for themselves but for him who died for them and was raised again."

The challenge for today: Understand that the Holy Spirit lives inside of us, and God wants our lives to be controlled by Him. We must face the crucial question of who controls our lives: Self or Christ. We must understand this before moving to the next step, "Submission." Lose control and fully surrender your heart and soul to Jesus Christ.

-32-
Who Do You Turn To?

No one has ever said life will be easy. We all have found that out the hard way. We will face many trials, heart-stopping situations, heartache, and difficulties. You will be talked about, persecuted, laughed at, and made fun of more than once. There will be seasons in this life when you want to throw up your hands and give up. How often do we fight for what is right and stand up for what we believe just to be knocked down and pushed aside? Do you ever feel overwhelmed, defeated, frustrated, and depressed? Do you ever feel alone and left behind by friends? How many of us struggle to pay our bills and barely get by each month? It seems to be a continuous cycle that never goes away. Who do you turn to when life slaps you in the face?

> Psalm 121:1-8: "I lift up my eyes to the hills-where does my help come from? My help comes from the Lord, the Maker of heaven and earth. He will not let your foot slip-he who watches over you will not slumber; indeed, he who watches over Israel will neither slumber nor sleep. The Lord watches over you-the Lord is your shade at your right hand; the will not harm you by day, nor the moon by night. The Lord will keep you from all harm-he will watch over your life; the Lord will watch over your coming and going both now and forever."

I serve a God who knows my strengths, and He knows my every weakness. He knows when I doubt and when I am struggling with my faith. He knows when I am tired and when and when I am down. He knows me, and He loves me anyway. He promises me that He will never leave me or forsake me. He never took His watchful eye off me and saw my every move. You see, God didn't save Daniel from the lion's den but saved Daniel in the lion's den. God doesn't get us out, but He gets us through. He is a God of deliverance and a God who adores you.

The challenge for today: Turn to the Lord; you can trust Him with everything you have. This includes the good, the bad, and the ugly. He will never turn His back on you and make a way, even when all seems hopeless. Cry out to your Heavenly Father, express your feelings, and get everything off your chest. Don't hold back; He wants to hear from you. Those who place their trust in the Lord will not be shaken. I pray for you to receive encouragement and peace today.

-33-
Banish Anxiety

Ecclesiastes 11:9-10: "Be happy, young man, while you are young, and let your heart give you joy in the days of your youth. Follow the ways of your heart and whatever your eyes see, but know that for all these things, God will bring you to judgment. So then, banish anxiety from your heart and cast off the troubles of your body, for youth and vigor are meaningless."

How many of us have said, "I would love to be young again." But have you ever stopped long enough to think that through? Yes, I would love to be able to run, jump, and throw a ball without hurting the following day. But to go back to that stage of life wouldn't be easy. Think about those days when you had to figure everything out; you had huge dreams but faced many disappointments. Everything seemed to be within your reach, but you discovered they were further away than you thought. Anxiety was high with all the pressures of life because you thought you had to figure everything out today.

Solomon said, "Banish anxiety from your heart and cast off the trouble of your body." Banish means to forbid, abolish, or get rid of. How do we banish anxiety? How do we get rid of worry in our lives? How do we abolish those things that weigh us down? We are all guilty of running unnecessary thoughts through our minds and thinking about things that may never come to pass. How much energy and brain cells do we waste daily worrying about what people think about us, or what if something terrible happens?

You banish anxiety by not continually looking or focusing on the problem. Take your eyes off the issue at hand and turn your eyes to the Lord. That sounds super religious and unrealistic, but look at what the Word of God tells us.

> *Psalm 121:1-2: "I left up my eyes to the hills-where does my help come from? My help comes from the Lord, the Maker of heaven and earth."*

> *Hebrews 12:2: "Let us fix our eyes on Jesus, the author and perfecter of our faith, who for the joy set before him endured the cross, scorning its shame, and sat down at the right hand of the throne of God."*

> *Matthew 6:25: "Therefore I tell you, do not worry about your life, what you will eat or drink; or about your body, what you will wear. Isn't life more important than food, and the body more important than clothes?*

The challenge for Today: Drop the weight of anxiety, worry, and depression. It's not worth it. Take your eyes off the misconceptions, lies, and depression. Then, turn your eyes to Jesus Christ. He will make your path straight. He can calm your spirit and bring peace to all the confusion in your life.

-34-
Clear the Room

Renovating an older house is never easy, and there is always something to do. We have completed many significant projects but still must attack the old, worn-out carpet in the master bedroom. When we were about to finish the bathroom renovation, Laura and I went to the local carpet shop and picked out the rug we both liked. Then they sent a representative to measure the room and give us a price. We agreed to move forward, and they ordered the carpet. A few days passed, and the new rug arrived at the store. The store manager called and said they could come the next day, but we would have to move all the furniture out. In other words, we had to clear the room. Nothing could be on the floor. My wife and I got to work.

The carpet store couldn't do their work until everything was out of the room. Piece by piece, we worked together to move the bed, nightstands, dresser, and shoes that covered our closet floor. Before we moved everything from the room, I felt like the carpet was in bad shape. Now that everything is out, I know it was super nasty. The carpet installers showed up right at 9:30 a.m. the following day. I showed them the master bedroom, and they got to work. They didn't waste any time and began to rip that old carpet out. In minutes, all that nasty carpet was out the door. After some cleanup, they carried in the new padding and carpet. They didn't mess around, and my beautiful new rug was in place. What a difference it made. That room took on a whole new appearance. It even smelled different.

Here is my question for you today. What is God asking you to do to clear the room of your heart? What is stopping Jesus from tearing out the old carpet of your life and replacing it with something so much better? It may be pride, shame, guilt, or selfishness.

> *Philippians 2:12-13: "My dear friends, as you have always obeyed-not only in my presence, but now much more in my absence-continue to work out your salvation with fear and trembling, for it is God who works in you to will and to act according to his good purpose."*

The challenge for Today: Work out your salvation with fear and trembling. Make your time with God your priority, and listen to what God says about your life. If we listen, He will tell us what needs to be moved out. It will take effort and may not be easy, but it will be worth it. Allow Him to rip out that nasty sin, that arrogant pride, and that dark stain of lust. Then, replace it with new hope, new peace, new joy, and fresh purposes. Clear the room; what are you waiting on?

-35-
At Just The Right Time

Romans 5:6-8: "At just the right time, when we were still powerless, Christ died for the ungodly. Very rarely will anyone die for a righteous man, though for a good man, someone might possibly dare to die. But God demonstrated his own love for us in this: While we were still sinners, Christ died for us."

At just the right time in God's perfect plan, Jesus endured the cross.

Matthew 27:27- 31: "Then the governor's soldiers took Jesus into the Praetorium and gathered the whole company of soldiers around him. They stripped him and put a scarlet robe on him, and they twisted together a crown of thorns and set it on his head. They put a staff in his right hand and knelt in front of him and mocked him. 'Hail, king of the Jews!' they said. They spit on him, took the staff and struck him on the head again and again. After that they mocked Him, they took off the robe and put his own clothes on him. Then they led him away to be crucified."

Can you imagine the pain and suffering that Jesus endured? Can you picture the size of those nails that pierced His hands and feet? What about the flogging that ripped His skin off His back and legs? Can you see the pain on Jesus's face as the spear pierced His side? Have you ever thought about what Jesus felt when the soldiers dropped the cross in the hole as He hung by three nails? At just the right time, Jesus died.

> *Matthew 28:1-7: "After the Sabbath, at dawn on the first day of the week, Mary Magdalene and the other Mary went to look at the tomb. There was a violent earthquake, for the angel of the Lord came down from heaven and, going to the tomb, rolled back the stone and sat on it. His appearance was like lightning, and his clothes were white as snow. The guards were so afraid of him that they shook and became like dead men. The angel said to the women, 'Do not be afraid, for I know that you are looking for Jesus, who was crucified. He is not here; he has risen, just as he said. Come and see the place where he lay. Then go quickly and tell his disciples: He has risen from the dead and is going ahead of you into Galilee. There you will see him.' Now I have told you."*

At just the right time, Jesus arose from the grave! This is the day we celebrate our risen Lord as believers in Jesus Christ. Our God is not dead, but He is alive and well. He overcame sin and death, and He is sitting at the Father's right hand. Jesus is the Giver of Life, the King of kings, and the Lord of lords. He is my personal Lord and Savior of my soul. We have a God who loves us and willingly gave His very best for our good. He is not mad at you, but He is mad about you.

He is knocking at your heart's door at just the right time. Will you open that door and receive the gift of life? He is calling you to Himself. He is there to forgive, cleanse, and love you. Let's celebrate our risen King! Let us honor Him with praise and glory today.

-36-
Will It Last?

I urge you to slow down enough to think about something today. Please don't read this and move on. I encourage you to take time to ask yourself some difficult questions. Have you ever noticed how fast life passes the older you get? The truth is that the sand of your hourglass of life will run out sooner than you think. With that thought in mind, here is the question I want you to answer. What have you done for Christ that will last forever?

One day, your life will come to a close. It could be twenty years from now, or it could be tomorrow. When that day comes, will you regret what you did with your life? What will you take with you into eternity? Will it be that lovely house you live in? Will it be all that money you saved for a rainy day? Will it be that King Cab truck that you have kept shining for so many years? How many of those things that captured your thoughts and energy will you keep forever? One hundred years from now, how would you wish you had used your life?

I plead with you today to make the next chapter of your life count. For the person close to retirement, do you want to spend the last fifteen years of your life before you meet Jesus on vacation? Are we living a life for God's glory or our selfish pleasure? Life is too short, eternity is too long, and the stakes are too high to waste your years. We only get a brief moment in time to impact all eternity. Please don't waste it. Eternity is real. The gospel is true. Every person's soul matters, and your life counts.

Romans 10:14-15: "How, then, can they call on him they have not believed in? And how can they believe without hearing about him? And how can they hear without a preacher? And how can they preach unless they are sent?"

Here is the reality: people without Jesus are headed to a tragic end, leading to hell. Do we, the Church, realize this world's lostness and the desperate need to share the Good News of Jesus? God wants every person alive to hear the gospel, urging the Church to make it happen. Live life with purpose. Invest in what lasts forever. Share Jesus and live life with passion.

-37-
The Call

Matthew 4:19: "Follow me," Jesus said, 'I will make you fishers of men.'"

That means when you accept Jesus, you get the call to the mission. The question is no longer if you are called, only where and how. We are called to leverage our lives for the Great Commission if we are in Christ. In Matthew 28:18-20, Jesus shared the disciples' marching orders before he ascended to heaven. This message was to be their purpose for living. This was Jesus' heartbeat and His call for His disciples' lives. I want you to hang on to this today: this is not optional if you are a born-again believer in Jesus Christ. Matthew 28:18-20 isn't called the Great Suggestion but the Great Commission.

Matthew 28:18-20 Jesus said, "All authority in heaven and on earth has been given to me. Therefore go and make disciples of all nations, baptizing them in the name of the Father and the Son and the Holy Spirit, and teaching them to obey everything I have commanded you. And surely I am with you always, to the very end of the age."

God is calling you out and setting you apart to be fishers of men. You are called to be the salt and the light where you live and work. You are called to be the difference maker and add the flavor of Jesus to everything you touch. Don't live to fulfill your bucket list, and stop dreaming of retirement. We have a message that we have to share with the entire world.

> *Matthew 9:37-38: "Then Jesus said to his disciples, 'The harvest is plentiful, but the workers are few. Ask the Lord of the harvest, therefore, to send out workers into his harvest field."*

"Lord, teach us to number our days, and help us to invest in things that will last forever." Don't take a minute for granted; take time to pour into the people's lives around you. Keep your eyes wide open to the needs around you. God has planted you right where you are for a reason. I challenge you today to share your story with someone who doesn't know Christ. Tell someone about the difference that Jesus has made in your life. By the way, don't forget to smile. God will use a smile to open a door of conversation with people you don't know.

-38-
Look For the Warning Signs

Since moving to Titusville, I have worked in my yard to get it up to standard. We have removed trees and old potted plants that weeds have overgrown, and I fixed numerous sprinkler heads. Blood, sweat, and tears have returned this yard to where it needs to be. I am finally in a place where I don't have to spend my entire day slaving in the yard. Hallelujah!

Since my yard looks much better, I stopped walking around and checking things out. House projects became my focus and consumed all my time. I placed the yard on the back burner and went into maintenance mode. For several weeks, I did the very minimum regarding yard work. I was very content with the outcome of my lawn; my wife and I take great pride in how good everything looks.

But that was about to change. Yesterday, we came home from grabbing dinner at Sonny's, and we noticed a patch of grass in the front yard that looked dry and lifeless. I jumped out of the car to check out the situation. What has happened to my green grass? Something was wrong because my sprinkler system was programmed to come on every day. My grass shouldn't be this dry. So, I admittedly went to my sprinkler controls and turned on that zone of the yard. The water sprinkler heads began to pop up, and I noticed a huge issue. The sprinkler head was busted, and the water was shooting straight up in the air. It wasn't hitting the dry glass at all.

Why didn't I notice this early? Why didn't I recognize this issue before now? Because I became content, I got busy doing other things that seemed more important. I ignored the warning signs and got distracted.

> *Proverbs 4:25-26: "Let your eyes look straight ahead, fix your gaze directly before you. Make level paths for your feet and take only ways that are firm."*

Have you become distracted in your walk with Jesus Christ? Have you found other things that have grabbed your attention and focus? Are there warning signs around you, but you choose to ignore them? Warning signs such as depression, sadness, and fear may be flashing, telling us something is wrong. I encourage you to keep your spiritual eyes open and look straight ahead. Fix your gaze on Jesus and glance at everything else. If you seem a little dry spiritually, stop what you are doing and survey your life. Don't be afraid to ask hard questions, and take steps to make the proper corrections. By the way, it's okay to ask for help. Pay close attention to the warning signs.

-39-
Get Discipline

Proverbs 13:24: "He who spares the rod hates his son, but he who loves him is careful to discipline him."

My brother and sister say I was the "Golden Child," but I disagree. That has been an ongoing joke for some time now. But according to this verse, they may be right. My dad must have loved me ten times as much as them because I was the one who got all those spankings. One thing is sure: I got my share of discipline on my backside. My dad wasn't scared to draw a line and tell me not to cross it. But he took the time to tell me what would happen when I did cross it. It took me a long time to learn, but I found out that my dad stood by what he said. I never claimed to be a faster learner.

One of the dumbest statements I ever heard my dad say was, "This is going to hurt me more than it's going to hurt you." That didn't make any sense at the time. Yes, I crossed that line. I knew what was coming but thought it might be worth the discipline. Boy, was I wrong? Then I responded to my dad's statement, "You must be a bad man because I am dying over here." The truth is, I deserved every bit of discipline I received from my parents. My parents disciplined me because they loved me. They punished me because they wanted me to learn how to treat people and live unselfishly. I had a lot to learn.

Hebrews 12:10-11: "Our fathers disciplined us for a little while as they thought best; but God disciplines us for our good, that we may share in his holiness. No discipline seems pleasant at the time, but painful. Later on, however, it produces a harvest of righteousness and peace for those who have been trained by it."

You may be walking through tough times, which doesn't make sense. God has drawn a line for us not to cross. Like me, you have crossed that line and know what is coming. Know this: God loves you, and because He loves you, He is not scared to discipline you. Keep in mind that He only wants what is best for you. Thank God for loving you enough to discipline you when you stray and run off doing your own thing. He is a good Father.

-40-
Plow the Fields

If you have ever studied church history, you know that often, a church will be great in one generation and falter in the next. Either they sat on their blessing and became comfortable, or they refused to obey the Father. More than ever, the Church of Jesus Christ must seek the Lord's face. Yes, we need to pursue His presence and pray boldly.

> *Matthew 9:35-38: "Jesus went through all the towns and villages, teaching in their synagogues, preaching the good news of the kingdom and healing every disease and sickness. When he saw the crowds, he had compassion on them, because they were harassed and helpless, like sheep without a shepherd. Then he said to his disciples, 'The harvest is plentiful, but the workers are few. Ask the Lord of the harvest, therefore, to send out workers into his harvest field.'"*

Jesus made an impact, and he engaged his community. I love this Scripture because it shows us the heart of Jesus. He cared about people and their situations. He lived with His eyes wide open to the people around him. He saw other people's hurt, pain, and suffering. Pause for a few seconds and ask yourself a few questions. What do you weep about? In other words, what breaks your heart? What is your holy discontent? What drives you? What motivates you, and what gets you out of bed every morning? What is your God-dream? What has God placed in your heart?

We will never make an impact in our comfort zone. You see, God is calling His Church to be comfortable with being uncomfortable. Have you ever been stuck in the routine of tradition? Has your walk with God and ministry become something you must do to be a good Christian? It has become stale and dry.

Fallow ground is unproductive and undisturbed. It must be broken up, and the rocks and weeds must be removed. The tilling must be deep because preparation is essential for a vast harvest. God is looking for that one man, woman, or Church that will dare to be different and is willing to step out on faith. It is time to plow the fields! It's time to put into action what we claim to believe.

Plowing is hard work, but it is worth it when you see the harvest. Die to selfishness and pride. Allow God to plow the field of your heart. Let Him go deep and produce a harvest in you. Don't allow tradition and routine to stop you from having a new and fresh relationship with Jesus. He is doing something new and fresh every day. Enjoy your walk with God, and let that motivate you to continue plowing. Let your time with God stir up the passion for ministry in your heart and push you to love others with the love of Christ. Keep plowing!

-41-
My Food

John 4:34: "My food," said Jesus, 'is to do the will of him who sent and to finish his work. Do you not say, 'Four months more and then the harvest'? I tell you, open your eyes and look at the fields! They are ripe for harvest."

Jesus says, "Open your eyes and look at the fields!" Did you notice the exclamation mark? Jesus had a mission, and he was passionate about it. I feel an urgency in his words, and I can sense his desire to carry on the work of God in his life. In other words, Jesus told the church today to open its eyes and see our schools. Open your eyes, Church, and see your community. Open your eyes and see the hurt, death, pain, and depression around you. We must be willing to storm the gates of hell to fight for our kids, students, and friends.

Mark 5:25-34: "A woman was there who had been subject to bleeding for twelve years. She had suffered a great deal under the care of many doctors and had spent all she had, yet instead of getting better, she grew worse. When she heard about Jesus, she came up behind in the crowd and touched his cloak, because she thought, 'If I just touch his clothes, I will be healed.' Immediately, her bleeding stopped, and she felt in her body that she was freed from her suffering. At once, Jesus realized that power had gone out from him. He turned around in the crowd and asked, 'Who touched my clothes?' 'You see the people crowding against you.' his disciples answered, and yet you can ask, 'Who touched me?' But Jesus kept looking around to see who had done it. Then the woman, knowing what had happened to her, came and fell at his feet and, trembling with fear, told him the whole truth. He said to her, 'Daughter, your faith has healed you. Go in peace and be freed from your suffering.'"

In the middle of a crowd, a woman who suffered severely was desperate. She possessed the kind of desperation that God was looking for. Not only was she desperate to get to Jesus, but she was also willing to act in faith. She worked her way through the crowd to touch the hem of his garment, and she was made new. She was healed. Throughout the Gospels, Jesus was attracted to those kinds of desperate people. What a powerful combination! We can't impact our community until we want to get to Jesus at any cost, be willing to step out on faith, and believe in God for the impossible.

The challenge for today: Is your heart entirely in tune with the Father? Are His passions your greatest desires? Do you possess the kind of desperation and faith that God is looking for to do work in your community and the lives of people around you? Make Jesus your number one priority, and live life with a purpose. Then watch how lives will be changed around you, and experience the miracles of God.

-42-
Desperate?

Mark 10:46-52: "Then they came to Jericho. As Jesus and his disciples and a large crowd were leaving the city, a blind man, Bartimaeus, was sitting by the roadside begging. When he heard that it was Jesus of Nazareth, he began to shout, 'Jesus, Son of David, have mercy on me!' Many rebuked him and told him to be quiet, but he shouted all the more, 'Son of David, have mercy on me!' Jesus stopped and said, 'Call him.' So they called to the blind man, 'Cheer up! On your feet!' He's calling you. Throwing his cloak aside, he jumped to his feet and came to Jesus. 'What do you want me to do for you?' Jesus asked him. The blind man said, 'Rabbi, I want to see.' 'Go,' said Jesus, 'Your faith has healed you.' Immediately, he received his sight and followed Jesus along the road."

We need to press through obstacles and opposition. I will be the first one to confess I am guilty. Too many times, we resemble the Rich Young Ruler more than Bartimaeus. We become satisfied, content, and comfortable. We want life on our terms. We want ministry on our terms. We don't want to be inconvenienced by the cross of Christ. But we can't impact our community until we become desperate for Jesus, no matter the cost. We need a spirit of urgency in the Church.

Mark 2:1-5: "A few days later, when Jesus again entered Capernaum, the people heard that he had come home. So many gathered that there was no room left, not even outside the door, and he preached the word to them. Some men came, bringing to him a paralytic, carried by four of them. Since they could not get him to Jesus because of the crowd, they made an opening in the roof above Jesus and, after digging through it, lowered the mat the paralyzed man was lying on. When Jesus saw their faith, he said to the paralytic, 'Son, your sins are forgiven.'"

The common thread in these two scriptures was that they were all desperate to get to Jesus. They didn't care what people thought and did whatever it took to get his attention. No risk was too great. Not only did Jesus see their desperation, but He also saw their great faith. What a powerful combination to have in our lives and the Church today. Are you desperate to get to Jesus? Is your faith soaring? I dare you to mix those two traits and see the power of God move in your life. Let's go.

-43-
Preparation for the Church

God is at work, and He is moving across this country. Lives are being changed, and I pray for a Holy Ghost Revival to sweep our nation. I am not praying for a scheduled revival service, where a visiting pastor comes and speaks at both services on Sunday and then returns each night till Wednesday night. I am praying for a mighty move of God to break out in my life and the life of the Church. "Lord, give your Church the strength to keep plowing and help us not to grow weary. Father, equip us to keep sowing the seeds of grace and love everywhere we go. Lord, send the rain of Your glory, the rain of Your love, and the rain of Your Holy Spirit." We can plow, plant, and even irrigate, but only God can send the rain.

Talking about it is not enough, but we must be prepared. We must put in the work. We have to be willing to plow the fields if we want to see a harvest. Four things need to take place in our lives to prepare ourselves for the mighty move of God.

1. Selfishness and pride have to go.

There is no room for division, broken relationships, and pride. Take time to read Matthew 18:15-35. It is time to go and make things right with those who have wronged you. That anger, hard feelings, and hostility are called sin. It is hindering your relationship with the God of the universe. Take time to ask God to forgive you and to cleanse you.

Then, ask God to give you the strength to walk in grace. It is time to advance His Kingdom!

2. We need to be desperate for Jesus.

Take a serious look at your priorities and how they line up. Does Jesus sit on the throne of your life, or does he have a seat at the back of the bus? What do you spend most of your time thinking about throughout the day? Church, Jesus needs to take His rightful place and be our number one priority. It is time to pursue His presence more than anything else.

3. There needs to be a spirit of expectancy and urgency in our hearts.

Not only do we need to pray to our Heavenly Father, but we need to pray boldly. I think we all forget how great our God is. He spoke the universe into existence and breathed life into us. People are dying daily without Jesus as their Lord and Savior; what are we doing about it? Stop putting off what God has placed in front of you to do. Now is the time.

4. Step out on faith and guard against unbelief.

Know God's Word and stand on His promises. It will not always be easy, but it will be worth it. That first step is always the hardest. But know this: take that first step, and He will help you walk it out.

Isaiah 43:18-19: "Forget the former things; do not dwell on the past. See, I am doing a new thing! Now it springs up; do you not perceive it? I am making a way in the desert and streams in the wasteland."

Today's takeaway: Set your heart right with the Lord. Take time to confess your sins to the Lord. Seek His face and hunger for His presence. Plow the field and stay with it. Don't become distracted. Push through the dry times. Pray for the rain of His Spirit to fall and expect a harvest of the Lord. It's all about the preparation. To God be the glory!

-44-
Getting Rid of the Clutter

We moved into our house in Titusville nearly ten months ago. Since then, we have transformed the yard, but I still have more work to do. We have also remodeled the kitchen and bathroom and replaced some nasty carpet with hardwood floors. It seems like a never-ending task. But there was one job I kept putting off for another day; I had to clean out the garage. The former owners left a ton of stuff on the shelves of our garage, and I have come up with many excuses to push this task off. It was much easier to avoid the mess and act like it wasn't that bad. The longer it sat there, the less it seemed to bother me.

Where do I begin? What needs to stay, and what needs to go? What will I use, or what needs to go in the trash? After a quick survey of the mess, Laura and I jumped into action, sorted through the clutter, and reorganized every shelf in the garage. The clutter had gotten so bad that finding the needed stuff took a lot of work. We filled up a trash can and the back of my pickup with unnecessary things. We just picked the hottest day of the year to tackle this undertaking. But it was worth it. I know where everything is, and I don't have to waste so much energy looking for a tool. My only regret was this: I wished I would have done it sooner.

Here are my questions to you: what is cluttering your life? What excuses are you telling God for putting off the cleanup process? Have you grown accustomed to all the junk lying around in the garage of your heart? Is there a sin you are avoiding and choose to overlook?

> *Psalm 139:23-24: "Search me, O God, and know my heart; test me and know my anxious thoughts. See if there is any offensive way in me, and lead me in the way of everlasting."*

The challenge for Today: Take some time and evaluate your life and passions. Slow down enough to listen to the God of the universe and what He is saying to you. Identify the things that are cluttering your heart and your passion for God. Ask God what needs to go and what needs to be reorganized. Then, obey what the Father is telling you. Your only regret is that you wish you had done this sooner. When we clean out the clutter of our hearts, God has an easier time finding tools He can use.

-45-
Do You Have Life Figured Out?

C an you recall those times when you seemed to have everything figured out? You knew exactly where you were going and how you would get there. You were going after your dream, and nothing would stop you.

I want to return to 1985, my senior year at Dougherty High School in Albany, Georgia. I knew exactly what I wanted. I wanted to marry my high school sweetheart, Laura Durham, and play professional baseball. Then I tried to become famous and make a lot of money. But life has a way of throwing us a curveball when we least expect it. I have never played professional baseball and am not rich or famous. But I did marry Laura Durham!

In my 55 years of life and over 30 years of ministry, I have seen a lot of heartache, difficulties, and struggles. I have watched moms and dads bury their precious children too early. I had a close friend struggle with diabetes and die before he got to see their grandbaby grow up. I had a couple of friends pass away unexpectedly, leaving everyone wondering what had just happened. I have seen cancer and disease destroy dreams and lifetime goals, and they were hoping to survive. I have seen parents' hearts break because of a wayward child struggling with addictions and bad habits. I have experienced how hard it is to overcome debt and monthly bills and live from paycheck to paycheck. What about lies that are spoken about you that destroy your good reputation? Things that don't make sense happen in this life that are totally out of your control.

We all hope for good days. We all dream of bright futures and endless happiness. We all want to ride off in the sunset with a smile, but tomorrow is coming, and we have no clue what it holds. Life as we know it can be changed in an instant. How do you deal with that? How do you handle the crazy turns and the ups and downs of life? When this world squeezes you, what comes out?

1 John 5:1-5: "Everyone who believes that Jesus is the Christ is born of God, and everyone who loves the father loves his child as well. This is how we know that we love the children of God: by loving God and carrying out his commands. This is love for God: to obey his commands. And his commands are not burdensome, for everyone born of God overcomes the world. This is the victory that has overcome the world, even in faith. Who is it that overcomes the world? Only he who believes that Jesus is the Son of God."

I don't know what tomorrow holds or what difficulties I will face. But I know I serve a God who holds tomorrow in His hands. And because I have a relationship with Jesus, I am an overcomer, and I will stand firm amid heartaches and disappointments. Greater is He that's in me than he that is the world. Do you have life figured out? True life can only be experienced through a relationship with Jesus Christ. Surrender your heart to the One who loves you the most, and give Him total control. He will hold you in the storms of life and bring you unexplainable peace.

-46-
Paul (The Real Deal)

Romans 10:1: "Brothers, my heart's desire and prayer to God for the Israelites is that they may be saved."

I love Paul's heart for the people of Israel. His passion and desire were to see them develop a personal relationship with Jesus. Paul seemed to be that guy who spoke what was on his mind even before thinking about how his words would affect the ones listening. He was strong, bold, and unashamed. Paul was always among the first to speak up and take the lead. He was a man of conviction, and he spoke God's words without hesitation. I admire how Paul walked with the Lord and loved the people around him. He was the real deal. He didn't try to win you with eloquent words or charm you with all his wisdom.

1 Corinthians 2:1- 5: "When I came to you, brothers, I did not come with eloquence or superior wisdom as I proclaimed to you the testimony about God. For I resolved to know nothing while I was with you except Jesus Christ and him crucified. I came to you in weakness and fear, and with much trembling. My message and my preaching were not with wise and persuasive words, but with a demonstration of the Spirit's power, so that your faith might not rest on men's wisdom, but on God's power."

To the Christian faith, Paul was the golden standard. But he was an ordinary person, just like us. He rolled out of bed every morning with body aches from a hard day's work, and he wondered what he would eat for breakfast. He dealt with life issues such as heartache, disappointment, and strife. Paul wasn't a fairytale character or a superhero cartoon figure but an ordinary man who loved God and the people around him. He had no clue that one day, millions of people would read the words that the Lord gave him. The Apostle Paul didn't do it for fame or recognition. He lived daily listening to the Father's voice and learned to pay close attention to what the Father was saying. Then he walked in obedience.

Paul faced a lot of pain and suffering for the cause of Christ. Have you ever wondered if he asked himself, "Is it worth it?" I am sure he did. But he stayed faithful and kept pressing forward, and he kept sharing the good news of Jesus. Because of his willingness to grind through life's difficulties, millions of people's lives are changed for all eternity. Stay faithful, and don't doubt the impact you are making for the cause of Christ. To God be the glory!

-47-
Salvation

Romans 1:16: "I am not ashamed of the gospel, because it is the power of God for the salvation of everyone who believes: first for the Jew, then for the Gentile."

The word salvation implies the idea of deliverance, safety, preservation, and healing. "Salvation" is the great inclusive word of the Gospel, connected to all the redemptive acts and processes: justification, redemption, grace, atonement, forgiveness, sanctification, and glorification. Salvation is in three tenses:

Justification:
1. **The Christian has been saved from the guilt and PENALTY of sin.**

    Ephesians 2:4-5 & 8-9: "But because of his great love for us, God, who is rich in mercy, made us alive with Christ even when we were dead in transgressions, it is by grace you have been saved. For it is by grace you have been saved, through faith-and this not from yourselves, it is the gift of God-not of works, so that no one can boast."

Sanctification:
2. **The Christian is being saved from the guilt and POWER of sin.**

Romans 6:14: "For sin shall not be your master, because you are not under the law, but under grace."

Galatians 2:19-20: "For through the law I died to the law so that I might live for God. I have been crucified with Christ, and I no longer live, but Christ lives in me. The life I live in the body, I live by faith in the Son of God, who loved me and gave himself for me."

Glorification:
3. **At the Lord's return, the Christian will be saved from all bodily infirmities resulting from sin. The Christian will be saved from the PRESENCE of sin.**

1 Corinthians 15:42-44: "So will it be with the resurrection of the dead. The body that is sown is perishable, it is raised imperishable; it is sown in dishonor, it is raised in glory; it is sown in weakness, it is raised in power; it is sown a natural body, it is raised a spiritual body."

Salvation is by grace through faith and is a gift from God, wholly without works. Have you experienced salvation through a relationship with Jesus? Have you ever confessed Him as Lord and Savior of your life? It's time to die to selfishness and pride. It's time to dethrone yourself from the throne of your heart and elevate Christ to His rightful place. It will be the greatest decision you will ever make.

-48-
Take Another Look

Our perspective: How we interpret what's happening can make or break us. Our perspective shapes us and determines how we think and react to people. Perspective creates opportunities to grow, or it hinders us as we walk through life. If our viewpoint leans towards the negative, we may be unaware of it. Thinking the worst can become second nature because we have been like this for so long.

The negative perspective says, I can't, or That is impossible. We tend to see the bad in people and every situation. The optimistic perspective says, I can, and I will. They choose to see the good in people and every situation. The faith-filled perspective says, I can do all things through Christ that strengthens me, and all things are possible with God. A faith-filled perspective says failure is a part of growth.

> Second Corinthians 4:18: "So we fix our eyes not on what is seen, but on what is unseen. For what is seen is temporary, but what is unseen is eternal."

God is calling His Church to enlarge our perspective, open our hearts from the vantage point of heaven, and see the world through the eyes of Christ. Then, we can see a whole new world that will change our lives and how we live. Trails and hard times will take on a whole new meaning. Our sense of purpose will be restored, and knowing God is in control will bring us hope and peace.

Colossians 3:2: "Set your mind on things above, not on earthly things."

Isaiah 55:8-9: "For my thoughts are not your thoughts, neither are your ways my ways,' declares the Lord. As the heavens are higher than the earth, so are my ways higher than your ways and my thoughts than your thoughts."

Life can be confusing, making us feel like we have been walking in circles. Maybe you have lost your perspective and are surrounded by the clutter of this world. Step back, turn to Jesus, and look from His perspective. Look at what matters in the eyes of the Lord, then invest in that.

Jeremiah 29:11-13: "For I know the plans I have for you," declares the Lord, 'plans to prosper you and not to harm you, plans to give you hope and a future. Then you will call upon me and come and pray to me, and I will listen to you. You will seek me and find me when you seek me with all your heart.'"

-49-
The Call

First Peter 1:13-16: "Therefore, prepare your minds for action; be self-controlled; set your hope fully on the grace to be given you when Jesus Christ is revealed. As obedient children do not conform to the evil desires you had when you lived in ignorance. But just as he who called you is holy, so be holy in all you do; for it is written: 'Be holy, because I am holy.'"

God has called every believer to a holy life. Holiness is not just for preachers, missionaries, and Sunday school teachers. If the truth is known, many Christians have cultural holiness; we adapt to the Christians around us. God hasn't called us to be like other Christians but commanded us to be like Jesus. Let that soak in today.

First John 1:5-7: "This is the message we have heard from him and declare to you: God is light; in him there is no darkness at all. If we claim to have fellowship with him yet walk in the darkness, we lie and do not live by truth. But if we walk in the light, as he is in the light, we have fellowship with one another, and the blood of Jesus, his Son, purifies us from all sin."

God is free from evil and is pure and holy. What about us? Does that question overwhelm you? It's a question we, as believers, need to be able to answer and not avoid. Think about it this way: God demands more than we acknowledge His holiness; He demands it to be evident in our lives. Have you ever tried to justify your actions, which our conscience calls into question? In other words, have we come up with excuse after excuse for hanging onto our sinful lifestyle?

Because God is holy, He hates sin. As we grow in holiness, we will grow to hate sin, too. Every time we sin, we are doing something God hates. The problem is that we all grow accustomed to our sins; we get used to them. Know this: God never ceases to hate sin. Our motivation for walking in holiness should be Jesus Christ and His great love for us. The righteousness of God is a high standard, but it is nevertheless one that He holds us to.

Is there a sin you need to confess? Is there selfishness that needs to be removed and replaced with a fruit of the Spirit? What habit do you need to turn over to the Lord? What about that secret sin you have been hiding for years? What is the Spirit shining His light on in your life as you read this devotion? Take action today! Give it to the Lord, confess your sins, and leave it at His throne of grace.

Jesus gave us a perfect example of how to live life. He is our go-by. He is the golden standard for living a life of holiness, not the guy next door. Pursue holiness and keep your eyes on Jesus. One thing is sure: we will mess up along the way, but let it be known who you are chasing after.

-50-
Whom Are You Imitating?

Second Corinthians 5:21: "God made him who had no sin to be sin for us, so that in him we might become the righteousness of God."

In this verse, we can see the holiness of Christ. He had no sin, and He lived the perfect life. He was the spotless lamb of God, and He willingly laid down His life at Calvary for us. When we see God's love for us, we understand how we missed the mark. In other words, He brings our sins into plain view. If we could understand the righteousness of Christ and that His righteousness is credited to us, it would change how we live.

Hebrews 4:15: "For we do not have a high priest who is unable to sympathize with our weakness, but we have one who has been tempted in every way, just as we are-yet was without sin."

Not only was Christ without sin, but He was also in perfect conformity to the will of God. Holiness has more to do than mere acts; our motives must also be holy. Have you ever served with the wrong motives or a bad attitude? Are our thoughts holy before Christ? Isaiah saw the holiness of Christ; look how he reacted.

Isaiah 6:5: "Woe to me!' 'I am ruined! For I am a man of unclean lips, and I live among a people of unclean lips, and my eyes have seen the King, the Lord Almighty.'"

We need to comprehend the holiness of Christ before we feel like Isaiah did. Part of growing in holiness is understanding that the Holy Spirit will make us aware of our need for holiness in our daily lives. Satan's job is to distract us from our focus on Jesus. Satan will do anything to wear you down, frustrate you, and cause doubt in your faith walk. He will tell you anything to keep you from pursuing holiness. Jesus is our ultimate example of how to live a life of holiness.

Ephesians 5:1-2: "Be imitators of God, therefore, as dearly loved children and live a life of love, just as Christ loved us and gave himself up for us as a fragrant offering and sacrifice to God."

The challenge for today: Ask the Lord to reveal your shortcomings, sins, and weaknesses. Take time to reflect, ask Him to cleanse you, and forgive you for falling short. Thank Him for His grace and mercies that He pours out on us daily. I also want to encourage you to study the life of Jesus, dig deep into scripture, and pattern your life after the Son of God. In all your thoughts, actions, and every part of your character, desire to follow Christ in doing the will of the Father.

-51-
Holiness in the Body

First Corinthians 9:27: "I beat my body and make it my slave so that after I have preached to others, I myself will not be disqualified for the prize."

Tru holiness involves more than just our hearts and our minds. It also includes control over our physical bodies and our appetites. We must recognize that our bodies are the temple where the Holy Spirit dwells. God created our bodies and our natural desires. However, if left uncontrolled, we will become instruments of wickedness.

Romans 6:13-14: "For if you live according to the sinful nature, you will die; but if by the Spirit you put to death the misdeeds of the body, you will live, because those who are led by the Spirit of God are sons of God."

First John 2:16-17: "For everything in the world-the cravings of sinful man, the lust of his eyes and the boasting of what he has and does-comes not from the Father but from the world. The world and its desires pass away, but the man who does the will of God lives forever."

I want to ask you a couple of questions to get you thinking. How often do we eat and drink, not because we are hungry or thirsty? How often do we lie in bed simply because we don't feel like getting up? How often do we give into that immoral and sinful lust?

> *Romans 12:1-2: "Therefore, I urge you, brothers, in view of God's mercy, to offer your bodies as living sacrifices, holy and pleasing to God-this is your spiritual act of worship. Do not conform any longer to the pattern of this world, but be transformed by the renewing of your mind. Then you will be able to test and approve what God's will is-his good, pleasing, and perfect will."*

We need to adopt an attitude of diligent obedience in every area of our lives. The Lord wants to see us grow in every area of life. I encourage you to guard against the spirit of laziness and indulgence of the body. We must learn to say no to our bodies instead of giving in to their desires and pursuits. Ask the Lord for strength and wisdom as you walk through this life. Commit to getting your heart rate up and stroll around the neighborhood. Watch what you eat, and learn to say no to that late-night ice cream. That last one may be tough. To God be the glory!

-52-
Game Plan

I played midget league football growing up in East Albany, Georgia. One year, I played on the Blackhawks, and we were undefeated. We all had a role to play; we knew our job and ensured we took care of our assignment. Plus, we had a kid named Curtis Smith. He was that kid who stood out, and nobody in the league could catch him. He was a touchdown machine! After every win, we would all get in the back of the coach's truck and ride to Burger King to eat. We would scream our cheers and our chants to the whole world. Can you imagine doing that today? We knew we would enjoy a grand celebration if we did our job.

What is your role in God's plan for your life? Where are you going? What is God asking you to do according to His Word? Are you doing your part? According to God's Word, we are called to serve others and love people to Jesus. I want to give you three things to think about today. Take time to run these things through your thoughts and see if God wants you to adjust how you spend your days.

- **First, make yourself available.**

When we serve others, we serve God. The number one thing needed to be a servant of God is availability. Yes, the ministry of presence, but business is the most prominent opponent of serving others. If the devil can't make you bad, he will make you busy. Take time to be still and meet with the Creator of the Universe. Slow down enough to hear the voice of the Holy God. Be open to following the impression of the Lord and ask Him to use you throughout the day. Look for ways to serve at your church, even for only one hour daily.

- **Secondly, meet the needs around you.**

   First Peter 4:10: "Each one should use whatever gift he has received to serve others, faithfully administering God's grace in its various forms."

Our God-given abilities have been given to us and are designed to serve others around us. They were not designed for us. Identify those gifts today, and take time to put them into action. For some people, you might have to dust them off. Nevertheless, take your eyes off yourself and open your spiritual eyes to the needs around you. I hate to oversimplify this, but when you see those needs, meet them.

   Jesus said this in Mark 10:45: "For even the Son of Man did not come to be served, but to serve, and to give his life as a ransom for many."

- **Last but not least, move people toward Jesus.**

Jesus met the people's physical needs to reach their spiritual shortcomings. Our goal isn't to be the savior but to do everything we can to help, encourage, and love people. It's not our calling to pull people out of sin but to push them toward Jesus Christ.

-53-
From Existing to Really Living
Part One

Where are you in your walk with Christ? What a question to ask at the beginning of a devotional. You would say you are doing fine if you are anything like me. There is nothing to jump up and down about, but I am doing well. I went to church for many years every time the doors were open. I taught Sunday School and served as a deacon on several committees. On the outside, I seemed to have the perfect Christian life. Yes, I was saved; there was no doubt about that. I was content to stay exactly where I had been for several years and didn't want to go further. I was in a spiritual rut and very comfortable in my faith walk.

I had a great job. Family and friends surrounded me. I was living in my two-story dream home, but something was missing. Have you ever had the feeling that there was something more? There had to be more to this life than what I was experiencing. I had everything I wanted but felt uneasy about my life. One morning, several years ago, I cried out to the Lord a straightforward prayer. I prayed and admitted that I was in a spiritual rut and tired of this mundane Christian life. I was tired of living safely and never trusting Him fully. That morning, I told the Lord I would give Him everything, no matter the cost. I surrendered everything, and the tears began to flow. A few moments went by, and it hit me. What did I pray? I can't believe those words came out of my mouth, but it felt so good. I didn't know then how much my life was about to change.

Maybe you are in that same spiritual rut that I was in. I dare you to stop what you are doing and ask yourself some questions. Am I just going through the motions of life? Am I going to church every Sunday to check a box? Am I experiencing excitement, passion, and joy when I wake up every morning? You keep yourself so busy and have so much going on that you lack the desire to spend time with the Lord. It took me a long time to learn this, but the following statement has a ton of truth. It's not about doing; it's about being. It doesn't matter who you are, but who you are.

What does God see when He looks at your heart? How big is your desire to be like Christ? Do you wake up each morning anticipating what the Lord will share? Are you tired of the same ole, same ole? Are you tired of working yourself to death in the church and never seeing any life change around you? Are you tired of just existing and not really living?

There is more to life than going to work and paying bills. There is more to life than collecting many toys and hoping you can one day retire and do what you want. I want to share three things the Lord showed me to pull me out of that spiritual rut. These three things gave me a new perspective and put passion back in my heart. Are you ready to go from existing to really living? More to come.

-54-
From Existing to Really Living
Part Two

Have you ever been stuck in life? Whether your car is stuck in the mud or life has bogged you down. Either way, being stuck is frustrating and will wear you down in time. Initially, we do everything we can to get unstuck, and we will try almost anything to break free. But as time passes, we become frustrated, tired, and reluctantly give up. We become content with our situation and decide to get used to our surroundings.

I want to encourage you to keep going. Break free from guilt, regrets, and thoughts holding you captive. It's time to walk in victory and not defeat. It's time to overcome and not be seduced by Satan's lies and schemes. It's time to live your best life and not feel like you are living to pay bills. I want to give you three things that will help you break free from the chains of darkness and set you on a new way of living. There are three steps to take to go from existing to really living.

- **Step One: Be honest with God and pour your heart out to Him.**

Tell Him your frustrations and your doubts. Tell Him about your struggles and confess those sins you have held on to for years. Hold nothing back, and make sure you express your darkest secrets, then leave it all at His feet, and don't pick it back up. No more living in fear and doubt.

Then, say to the Father, "I surrender all." What is stopping you from saying these words? What is preventing you from being sold out to Jesus?

- **Step Two: Self has to die.**

Self will do everything it can before it dies. Self will sing in the choir. Self will teach and do a great job. Self will go to church, and self will even preach.

> *Galatians 2:20: I have been crucified with Christ, and I no longer live, but Christ lives in me. The life I live in the body, I live by faith in the Son of God, who loved me and gave himself for me."*

When we accept Christ as our Lord and Savior, He comes and abides on the throne of our hearts. He comes to rule and reign. Over time, selfishness and pride begin to battle for the throne of our hearts. We are called to put whatever belongs to our old earthly nature to death. We are called to rid ourselves of anger, rage, malice, slander, and filthy language. Don't stop there, but make sure to put on the things of God. Clothe yourself with compassion, kindness, humility, gentleness, and patience. Make sure to read Colossians 3:5-17.

- **Step Three: Be full of the Holy Spirit.**

> *John 7:37-39 Jesus said, "If anyone is thirsty, let him come to me and drink. Whoever believes in me, as the Scripture has said, streams of living water will flow from within him."*

We are to thirst for more of Jesus. We are to desire Him more than anything else in our lives. We are called to come and drink from His heavenly straw. Yes, we are called to participate and receive from the very Spirit of God. Then believe. We, as believers, are called to be a container, a temple for the Holy Spirit to dwell. Know this: He is alive in you. Christ in me, the hope of all glory!

Today is the day to overcome and walk in the newness of life. It's time to tell the Lord I am tired of living a dull, humdrum life. Tell Him today, "I want more." Are you tired of doing church and ready to run the race God has for you? Seek His face more than you seek His hands. Come to a place where you are dependent on your Heavenly Father. God is calling you to a victorious Christian life. What are you waiting on? Take these three steps today, and prepare to live a peaceful, contentment, and passionate life. Let's go!

-55-
Standing at a Crossroads

L ife is full of choices. You have to choose what clothes you will wear each day, what you will eat, what toothpaste to use, and whether or not you will obey God. Making choices is a part of life; our choices affect us and the people around us. Have you ever heard the phrase "Standing at a Crossroads?" What pops into your head when you hear this phrase?

I think about our great country in 1963 when John F. Kennedy was assassinated. I also think about when a man walked on the moon in 1969 and the terrorist attacks on Washington, DC, on September 11, 2001. These events were game-changers in our country and all around the world. What about the Covid epidemic in 2020? All these events are defining moments; they are turning points in our nation's history. Can you think of any defining moments in the history of your local body of believers? How about your walk with the Lord? What life events stick out, those defining moments that have shaped your relationship with the Lord?

A great example in the Old Testament of a people standing at a crossroad can be found in Exodus. God called Moses to lead His people out of Egypt. He faced a challenging situation, but Moses obeyed what God called him to do. It wasn't easy, and Moses wasn't always willing. He had to face his fears, insecurities, and his inadequacies. But when Moses finally led the children of Israel out of Egypt, they found themselves in the desert, and Pharaoh's army pursued them. They were in an impossible situation.

Over the years, I have found out that's when God does His best work. I want to share with you three points about a defining moment:

A defining moment often challenges us to move from the known to the unknown. What is it about the unknown that scares us? Are we worried that God may call us to do something we are not qualified to do? Or will He ask us to go someplace we don't want to go? As Christians, we love to play it safe. We love to trust in ourselves and not God. A defining moment often challenges us to move from standing still to action. Have you ever noticed that when God's people face a great challenge, there are always well-meaning people who ask to stand still? Walking into a challenging situation requires divine power and a human response.

When we do what we can, God does what only God can do. A defining moment often challenges us to move from doubt to faith. There is a time to pray, but there is also a time to take God at His Word. That first step is always the hardest to take when facing a difficult situation. God may be calling you to something that doesn't make sense, and you are scared to death. You may face an impossible situation, and God tells you to move forward. Never forget that there is divine protection when God tells you to move forward. Does that mean you will have immunity against all difficulties? No, but the will of God will not lead you where the grace of God will not sustain you. Defining moments become turning points that affect the moment and the future. What will you do with your defining moment?

Philippians 1:6: "Being confident of this, that he who began a good work in you will carry it on to completion until the day of Christ Jesus."

-56-
A Call to the Ordinary

First Corinthians 1:26-29: "Brothers, think of what you were when you were called. Not many of you were wise by human standards; not many were influential; not many were of noble birth. But God chose the foolish things of the world to shame the wise; God chose the weak things of the world to shame the strong. He chose the lowly things of this world and the despised things-and the things that are not-to nullify the things that are, so that no one may boast before him."

Jesus became tremendously popular among the people of Galilee; he performed many miracles, so many people came to see Him in action. When the crowds reached their peak, Jesus preached a bold message confronting the people's hearts. Then, the multitude began to melt away.

John 6:66-67: "From this time, many of his disciples turned back and no longer followed him. 'You do not want to leave, too, do you?' Jesus asked the Twelve."

Among them who stayed with Christ were the twelve disciples. Jesus personally chose these men himself. Jesus didn't select a rabbi, scribe, pharisee, or priest. He didn't choose anyone seminary trained, but He chose the fishermen, tax collectors, and other ordinary men. Twelve working-class men turned the world upside down for Jesus.

It wasn't because of their talents, intellectual abilities, political influence, and especially not their social status. It was because God worked in them to get it done. God chooses the humble, the lowly, and the meek. It's not the man, but the power of God in the man.

Acts 4:13: "When they saw the courage of Peter and John and realized that they were unschooled, ordinary men, they were astonished, and they took note that these men had been with Jesus."

The twelve disciples turned the world upside down, but Jesus had His hands full. These ordinary men were slow to believe, foolish, self-absorbed, self-centered, self-promoting, and very proud. They needed more faith and commitment and to be faster to understand. What does that sound like? Have you ever wondered why Jesus didn't pick a different group of men? No one could look back at this group of guys and conclude they did it in their abilities.

In Second Corinthians 12:9, Jesus said, "My grace is sufficient for you, for my power is made perfect in weakness."

Yes, we are all common people and have our weaknesses. But God is calling us to be extraordinary because of the Holy Spirit that lives in the heart of every believer. I want to challenge you to dream big but pray bigger! It is not about who you are, but it is all about who you are. You are the child of the Living God—Christ in me, the hope of all glory. Let's turn the world upside down for the glory of God.

-57-
Fan the Flame
Part One

Second Timothy 1:4-6: "Recalling your tears, I long to see you, so I may be filled with joy. I have been reminded of your sincere faith, which first lived in your grandmother Eunice and, I am persuaded, now lives in you also. For this reason I remind you to fan into flame the gift of God, which is in you through the laying on of my hands."

We find Paul imprisoned again, only being freed for five years. Paul was placed in a dungeon, and his only contact with the outside world was an eighteen-inch square in the ceiling of his cell. I have always admired Paul's boldness and confidence. I see him being a loud person who always speaks what is on his mind, even if it gets him in trouble. The book of Second Timothy records Paul's last will and testament. In this letter to Timothy, Paul has no words of regret. He was at peace with God and how he lived his life. If I could summarize the book of Second Timothy, it would be Paul encouraging Timothy to keep on. I don't know about you, but that is a message I need to hear today.

In verse six, Paul encourages Timothy to "stir up the gift of God." In other words, keep the gift of God in full flame. I love sitting around a fire when it is cold. Watching the wood burn and feeling the warmth on my face is so relaxing. But what if we get sidetracked and ignore the flame? That flame will die down. As believers in Jesus

Christ, we are getting sidetracked and missing God's flame in our lives. Yes, we go to church and check off a box every Sunday, but we find ourselves just going through the motions. We get caught up in the craziness of life, and we take our eyes off what is most important: the flame of God.

Let me poke around a bit and ask you some questions. Are you excited about going to church every Sunday? Do you go to church expecting God to do great things? Do you ever pray for God to bless the people who will be there? Are you excited about getting up every morning to hear what God has for you today? Does your fire and passion for God need to be stoked in your heart?

It's time to rise from our spiritual slumber! Get ready to stir up the fire of God in your life, throw some gas on your spiritual flame, and confess the sin of contentment to God the Father. Satan has rocked the Church to sleep, and we are guilty of watering down the Gospel of Jesus Christ. Remember, there is power in the name of Jesus! Can you recall the feeling when you received Jesus into your heart? Can you recall that excitement, that peace, and that joy you had when Christ sat on the throne of your life?

How do I fan the flame of God in my life? To be continued tomorrow.

-58-
Fan the Flame
Part Two

I want to give you three things to help you fan the flame of God in your life. But I also want to pray and ask God to refresh you, restore you, and give you a spirit of encouragement that will engulf your entire being. Take the time to push away the negative things that are overwhelming you, and thank God for all the blessings of life you are taking for granted. Then, watch how your flame will begin to grow. Here are three things that need to take place to poke the fire of God in your life.

1. **Return to your first love.**

   Revelation 2:5: "Remember the height from which you have fallen! Repent and do the things you did at first. If you do not repent, I will come to you and remove your lampstand from its place."

God desires to have fellowship with us, and He is standing there with His arms open wide. It's time to repent of our sins and selfishness. It is time to get our priorities in order and give the throne of our lives. Yes, this means we need to recommit our lives to Christ.

2. **Get rooted in the Word, and bathe everything in prayer.**

Hebrews 4:12: "For the word of God is living and active. Sharper than any double-edged sword, it penetrates even to dividing soul and spirit, joint and marrow; it judges the thoughts and attitudes of the heart."

Ask God to give you a hunger for His Word. The Word of God will convict you of sin, encourage and uplift you, and hold you steady in the storm. Push away the excuses Satan feeds you daily for not digging into His Word. Fill your mind with the words of the Lord. Fill your mind with the things of God. Then pray. God has given us the gift of prayer, and we have the privilege of going to the very One who hung the moon and the stars in place. There is power in prayer, the gateway to constant fellowship with the Father.

3. Keep fighting, and don't give up.

Ephesians 6:10-13: "Finally, be strong in the Lord and in his mighty power. Put on the full armor of God so that you can stand against the devil's schemes. For our struggle is not against flesh and blood but against the rulers, against the authorities, against the powers of this dark world, and against the spiritual forces of evil in the heavenly realms. Therefore, put on the full armor of God, so that when the day of evil comes, you may be able to stand your ground and, after you have done everything, to stand. Stand firm."

Raise awareness of what is happening around you and your family. We are fighting a spiritual war. Don't allow Satan to get the best of you. Church, it is time to fight back and stand our ground. When Satan turns up the heat, don't back down, and don't give up. But fan the flame of God and watch it grow! Lean on the Holy Spirit that lives inside of you.

I want to encourage you to return to your first love. Get your heart right with the Lord, and confess your shortcomings. Dive into the Word of God and cover everything you do in prayer. Then, keep fighting and don't give up. You will overcome!

-59-
Personal Note

Ihave always been a dreamer, and I have always encouraged others to dream, too. My motto for life was this: Dream big. I will not bore you with all the crazy thoughts I have had over the years. But God has been showing me so many things over the last couple of days that He has caused me to add something to my motto for life. Something has been missing. My motto needed to be completed, and my dreams never came true. Have you ever felt like you were coming up short or that you might have been dreaming too small? Have you ever struggled in life, and it seems everybody else is taking off? You are not alone; we all deal with this sooner or later.

> *Acts 2:17: "In the last days, God says, 'I will pour out my Spirit on all people. Your sons and daughters will prophesy, your young men will see visions, your old men will dream dreams.'"*

I fall into the category of the older man. It is weird to say this, but it is true; I only have a third of my life left if I am lucky. I see it like this: so much to do in such a short period of time. God has filled me with many God dreams; sometimes, they overwhelm me, and I become frustrated. Sometimes, I wonder if I am just crazy, or must I be more realistic and settle for a good, everyday life? But God showed me to keep pushing, growing, and dreaming. Don't stop following my heart's passion, and don't stop seeking the presence of God.

That was when I felt God leading me to change my motto and take my dreams to a deeper level. He still calls me to dream but challenges me to pray bigger. Dream big, pray bigger! What a revelation. For years, I have been dreaming of God's dreams and trying to accomplish them with strength, wisdom, and effort. No wonder I came up short. No wonder I stay so frustrated. God showed me that my dreams would never exceed the prayers of my heart, spoken to the living God. It is time to step up my prayer life. It is time to depend on His strength and wisdom. I no longer have to worry about the results or outcome of any situation.

Keep following the passion that God has placed in you. Then drop to your knees, pray that the Father will prepare you, and go before you. Dream big, pray bigger! Change this world one person at a time.

-60-
Empty?

Luke 1:53: "He has filled the hungry with good things, but he has sent the rich away empty."

Even though your life is full of stuff, is something missing? Have you ever said, "There has to be something more to life than what I am experiencing?" Only if we admit we are empty can we be filled by Jesus. So many people come to church, but they will walk away empty. Most people have heard of Jesus but die having never really heard from Jesus. There is a vast difference. It saddens me to say this, but most people don't deny Him, yet they never rely on Him. That is the same as rejecting Him.

In Matthew 12:30, Jesus said, "He who is not with me is against me, and he who does not gather with me scatters."

Colossians 1:16: "For by him all things were created: things in heaven and on earth, visible and invisible, whether thrones or powers or rulers or authorities: all things were created by him and for him."

No one or nothing should take precedence over Jesus; if so, that becomes our idol. Our entire life will be out of order if Christ isn't first. I know that is a bold statement, but it is the truth. What are you chasing after? What this world has to offer will satisfy you for a time, but it will leave you empty and unsatisfied. It will leave you wanting more. God has created you to live by His truth, and when we don't, He designed depression as a warning sign. Depression to the soul is like a fever to the body. It is a sign that something serious is going on. The sad part is this: most people can't get their eyes on Jesus because they refuse to take their eyes off themselves.

The challenge for today: What are you pursuing and chasing after? What consumes your thoughts? Are you struggling with depression? I encourage you today to take your eyes off yourself and turn your focus to the very Creator of the universe. Spending time with Jesus helps us to gain the proper perspective. Be thankful instead of worrying, grumbling, and complaining about what you don't have. Take time to praise Him for the blessing of life and the gift of salvation only found in a love relationship with Jesus. Place Him on the throne of your heart. In other words, make Him the number one priority in your life, then watch how the motives of your heart begin to change. Come to His buffet table, eat, and enjoy the fullness you have been searching for.

-61-
Yes, and Amen

We all have those times when we must tear down the walls we have allowed to exist. We all fall short, and we all mess up. But having a God who understands and shows us so much grace is good. "Thank you, Lord, for the gift of forgiveness and mercy. Thank you for lifting me and encouraging me daily. Thank you, God, for the privilege of coming before you when I need to say I am sorry. Thank you for tearing down that old wall of sin in my heart." Yes, be thankful, but this is just the beginning of what God has for us as children of God. Not only does God want to break down the old walls of our lives, but He also wants us to build a solid foundation. A foundation that is solid and will stand firm even when the worst storms come our way.

> Matthew 7:24-25 Jesus tells us, "Therefore everyone who hears these words of mine and puts them into practice is like a wise man who built his house on the rock. The rain came down, the streams rose, and the winds blew and beat against that house; yet it did not fall, because it had its foundation on the rock."

What is your life built on? Before I go any further, I want to ensure you have a personal walk with Jesus Christ. Has there been a time in your life when you have come face to face with Jesus? Have you had an encounter with the Living God of the universe? Being a Christian and a Christ follower isn't about our church attendance. It is not about doing good deeds or being morally good. It's about a personal love relationship with Jesus and making Him the foundation on which everything is built. It is knowing that the eternal God made a way for us to come to Him. It is knowing and believing that He gave us His one and only Son to die on an old, rugged cross and believing Jesus didn't stay in that grave. This foundation is alive and well today, knowing that Jesus overcame sin and death. "Thank you, Lord!"

> *Revelations 3:20 says this, "Here I am. Behold, I stand at the door and knock. If anyone hears my voice and opens the door, I will come in and eat with him, and he with me."*

Have you answered that knock? Have you given your life to Jesus? Have you told Him, "Thank you" for what He has done for you? Have you ever asked him to come in and take over? Here is where it all begins.

-62-
A Life-Changing Relationship

Have you ever felt the power of God in your life? When was the last time you had something happen in your life that could only be explained by the work of the Holy Spirit? When was the last time you opened your Bible, and the words seemed to jump off the page and speak to you personally? When was the last time you worshipped and got lost in His presence? Has it been a while? God has called us to a life-changing relationship with Him through Jesus Christ. And that relationship changes everything.

> *Second Corinthians 5:17: "Therefore, if anyone is in Christ, he is a new creation; the old has gone, the new has come."*

There is a vast difference between religion and relationships. God doesn't call us to more religion. He calls us to an intimate relationship. Religion is activity; a relationship is intimacy. Religion is also words and works; the relationship is a walk. How many churches are filled with good, hard-working people but fail to have a personal relationship with the One who designed them? Their lives are nice, and they are not rocking any boat. But God has so much more intended for them. We all have an empty religious ritual when we go through the motions without meaning.

I encourage you to avoid getting caught up in the trap of doing. Don't allow your time with God to become a ritual or something you are supposed to do. Your relationship with the Lord should be close and intimate. Your time with God should be something you look forward to and a time to be fueled with His love. Surrender your entire being to Christ, and watch how He will radically change your mission and your meaning in life. Our weaknesses can be used for His glory when we abide in Him. He is calling you to a life-changing relationship with Him through Jesus Christ.

-63-
Growing in Holiness

Second Corinthians 7:1: "Since we have these promises, dear friends, let us purify ourselves from everything that contaminates body and spirit, perfecting holiness out of reverence for God."

Growing in holiness doesn't come naturally and is not easy. There will be struggles along the way, and you will learn much about yourself on the journey. Peter the Great said, "I have conquered an empire, but I have not been able to conquer myself." It is time to roll up our sleeves and get to work. I will not give you any profound theology-just straightforward, commonsense instructions about daily living in holiness.

Second Timothy 2:19-22: "Everyone who confesses the name of the Lord must turn away from wickedness." In a large house there are articles not only of gold and silver, but also of wood and clay; some are for noble purposes, and some for ignorance. If a man cleanses himself from the latter, he will be an instrument for noble purposes, made holy, useful to the Master, and prepared to do any good work. Flee from the evil desires of youth, and pursue righteousness, faith, love and peace, along with those who call on the Lord out of a pure heart."

The Lord requires four key actions from all who desire to be holy and prepared for every good work of Christ.

133

1. **Depart from iniquity. (Leave sin.)**
2. **Cleanse himself. (Leave old, unholy ways.)**
3. **Flee youthful lusts. (Leave your selfish desires.)**
4. **Pursue righteousness. (Chase after holiness.)**

The first half of holiness focuses on leaving something behind-departing from sin and fleeing lust. The second part of holiness focuses on chasing after something righteous.

> *Hebrews 12:1-2: "Therefore, since we are surrounded by such a great cloud of witnesses, let us throw off everything that hinders and the sin that so easily entangles, and let us run with perseverance the race marked out for us. Let us fix our eyes on Jesus, the author and perfecter of our faith, who for the joy set before him endured the cross, scorning its shame, and sat down at the right hand of the throne of God."*

Ask yourself a few questions, and then ask the Lord for wisdom. First, what do you need to put off or leave behind? What scheme does Satan use on you repeatedly to trip you up? What sins do you need to confess to the Lord? Then ask yourself, what am I chasing after? What do I have my eyes set on, and what controls my mind and consumes my time? I want to encourage you to flee from temptation, lust, and the snares of the Devil. Satan is good at what he does and knows how to attack you. Then, pursue righteousness and run after the things of God with everything you have. When you move toward holiness, you no longer seek to defend or rationalize your sin. The greater your desire for holiness, the more eager you become to be thoroughly cleaned and have a clean conscience before the Lord.

-64-
Unclog the Drain

A clogged drain is messier and aggravating, especially the sinks in the bathroom. Over time, different things fall into the sink and find their way down the drain. The collection of objects builds up, clogs the drain, and stops the water flow. Because of the buildup, the water begins to back up in the sink. Then you jump into action and grab the Drano, clothes hanger, or whatever you think will free the blockage. All we want is for the water to flow through the drain again.

Here is my question: how is the flow of the Spirit in your life? Is there sin clogging up the spiritual drain and not allowing the flow of God to move in your life? The greatest hindrance to the flow of God isn't a problem of motivation but one of accumulation. Christians often experience frustration and defeat in their spiritual lives due to a nasty buildup of unconfessed sin.

First John 1:9: "If we confess our sins, He is faithful and just to forgive our sins and to cleanse us from all unrighteousness."

Unconfessed sin blocks God's flow and movement in our lives, but confession is the tool we need to free up our spiritual drain and end our frustration and aggravation. We need a good spiritual cleaning and experience freedom and joy again in our relationship with Jesus. I encourage you to follow this simple ten-step spiritual cleansing process and spend time with it.

1. Find a quiet place to sit alone for at least one hour with a sheet of paper, something to write with, and your Bible.
2. Quiet your heart before the Lord by sitting still. Leave your phone in another room and push aside all distractions.
3. Pray to the Lord and thank Him for bringing you to this place. Let the Lord know you are committed to getting your heart right with Him and unclogging your spiritual drain.
4. Ask Him to reveal your sins one by one.
5. Begin to list everything the Holy Spirit reveals to you. Don't ignore the difficult ones.
6. Confess your sins one at a time to the Lord. Go through your list no matter how many sins you have listed. Tell Him how sorry you are, and ask Him to forgive and cleanse you.
7. Anticipate the personal struggle you will face. Fight the desire to run away and forget this whole process.
8. Make restoration wherever necessary and expect to humble yourself to at least one person.
9. Write done on your paper. Receive the Father's forgiveness and grace. Yes, say it out loud to your Heavenly Father.
10. Tell the Lord thank you for forgiving and showing you so much grace. Thank Him for cleansing your spiritual drain and allowing the flow of the Spirit to move in your life once again. Praise Him for His endless love, and enjoy His fellowship.

-65-
The Necessity of Repentance

What is repentance? It's acknowledging our sins to the Lord and agreeing that we have fallen short of Him. It also means we must change our behavior, attitude, and actions. Take time to read Second Samuel chapters eleven and twelve, and you will see how King David committed adultery, treason, and murder. When he thought he had covered it all up, Nathan, the prophet, confronted David about his sin. Then and there, David experiences conviction and acknowledges his sin. Genuine repentance is the key to spiritual breakthrough. Maybe you are struggling to hear from the Lord, and it seems like He is so far away. We all have been there at one time or another, so what must occur? I want to give you four steps that will free you up to experience that close, steady walk with the Father once again. Look at Psalm 51 and see David's actions to experience intimate fellowship with God again.

- **First, David acknowledged his sins.**

  Psalm 51:1-4: "Have mercy on me, O God, according to your unfailing love; according to your great compassion blot out my transgressions. Wash away all my iniquity and cleanse me from my sin. For I know my transgressions and my sin is always before me. Against you, you only, have I sinned and done what is evil in your sight."

Confess your sins to the Lord today. Please don't put it off. Take time to name them one by one.

- **Second, David sought the removal of his sins.**

Psalm 51:7-9: "Cleanse me with hyssop, and I will be clean; wash me, and I will be whiter than snow. Let me hear joy and gladness; let the bones you have crushed rejoice. Hide your face from my sins and blot out all my iniquity."

Forgiveness takes away sin, which results in the removal of guilt and shame. Too many Christians live defeated lives because they beat themselves up and hang on to their sins. Satan is loving every minute of it. After you ask for forgiveness, ask God to cleanse you.

- **Third, David trusted God to renew him.**

Psalm 51:10-12: "Create in me a pure heart, O God, and renew a steadfast spirit within me. Do not cast me from your presence or take your Holy Spirit from me. Restore to me the joy of your salvation and grant me a willing spirit, to sustain me."

Only God can take sinners and transform them into people of spiritual purity. God calls us to repent. Now trust God to renew you with the joy of His salvation. He is faithful, just, and willing to forgive us of all unrighteousness.

- **Finally, David maintained a readiness to repent.**

Psalm 51:15-17: "O Lord, open my lips, and my mouth will declare your praise. You do not delight in sacrifice, or I would bring it; you do not take pleasure in burnt offerings. The sacrifice of God is a broken spirit; a broken and contrite heart, O God, you will not despise."

As believers, we are to live humbly, aware of our tendency to sin. A new life in Christ begins today! Do you need a spiritual breakthrough? Then, set aside time with the Lord and talk it out. Then, get ready to experience that closeness with God once again.

-66-
The Struggle

Years ago, Billy Graham wrote a story about an old fisherman who came into town every Saturday afternoon. He always brought his two dogs with him. One dog was white, and the other was black. He had taught them to fight on command. Every Saturday afternoon in the town square, all the guys would gather, and these two dogs would fight, and the fisherman would take bets. On one Saturday, the black dog would win; another Saturday, the white dog would win-but the fisherman always won. His close friends began to ask him how he did it. He said, "I starve one and feed the other. The one I feed always wins because he is stronger." That is a harsh story, but it illustrates how we function as believers in Christ.

This illustration of the two dogs tells us something about the inner warfare that comes into the life of a person born again. We have two natures within us, both struggling to have control. Which one will dominate us? It depends on which one you feed. If we provide our spirit, man, and allow the Holy Spirit to empower us, He will rule over us. But if we starve our spirit man and instead feed the old, sinful nature, the flesh will dominate and win out. There is a spiritual battle going on within you 24 hours a day.

Romans 7:15 Paul says, "I do not understand what I do. For what I want to do. I do not do, but what I hate I do."

Galatians 5:17: "For the flesh sets its desire against the Spirit, and the Spirit against the flesh, for these are in opposition to one another, so that you may not do the things that you please."

As a believer in Christ, sin no longer reigns but still fights. Jesus has given me a new life, and He is in me to break the old habits, purify my motives, and set my eyes on more meaningful goals, especially becoming more like Christ. But remember that there will always be a struggle in the physical world and within you. Satan never gives up, and he will continue to attack your weaknesses. The enemy loves to appeal to our lust and our prideful hearts. But the good news is this: Greater is He that is in you than he who is in the world. In other words, if we cooperate with Him and turn to Him for help, He will give us the power to resist temptation. He will make us stronger due to every test that comes our way.

Which "dog" are you feeding, the spirit man or the natural man? The one that you feed always wins. I encourage you to feed that spiritual man, pull up to God's buffet line, and dive into God's Word. Take in His goodness, His wisdom, and His endless love. Fill your mind with truth; there will be less room for lies and lust. Practice God's presence and realize that the Holy Spirit lives inside you 24 hours daily. He never leaves us or forsakes us. Don't grow tired of doing good and following the Lord. Keep fighting and never back down. The Lord will give you everything you need to win and overcome.

-67-
Our Cry to God

We all have two spiritual needs. One is for forgiveness, and the other is for goodness. God heard our first cry for help and forgiveness and answered it at Calvary. God sent His Son, who knew no sin, to die on an old, rugged cross and overcome sin and death to bring us the gift of salvation. It is for everyone who reaches out and accepts God's gift by receiving Jesus as Lord and Savior.

God also heard our cry for goodness and answered it at Pentecost. God doesn't want us to come to Christ by faith, live a life of defeat and discouragement, and be overwhelmed by this world. He gave us the gift of the Holy Spirit. The Holy Spirit is the source of power that meets our needs, helps us to escape Satan's traps and temptations, and helps us live a victorious life.

If you believe in Jesus Christ, power is available to you that can change your life forever. The Holy Spirit will empower you, your family, and your ministry. This same power can transform your tired and lifeless church into a vital and growing body of believers. Unfortunately, this power has been ignored, misunderstood, and left out of many American churches today.

Peter said in Acts 2:38-39, "Repent and be baptized, every one of you, in the name of Jesus Christ for the forgiveness of sins. And you will receive the gift of the Holy Spirit. The promise is for you and your children and all who are far off, whom the Lord our God will call."

This is the great news: we are no longer waiting for the Holy Spirit-He is waiting on us. Praise God; we are no longer living in a time of promise but in the days of fulfillment. "Thank you, Lord!" The Holy Spirit was promised and fulfilled, the disciples were changed, and is present to every believer today.

Are you tired of being tired? Does your walk with God seem boring and lifeless? Do you long for a fresh encounter with the living God? Do you ever feel like you are going through the motion of worship and caught in a holy ritual, not a personal love relationship? Take time to thank God for the gift of salvation through the blood of Jesus Christ. Confess your sins to your Heavenly Father and thank Him for His grace. Ask the Father to cleanse you from all unrighteousness and to fill you with the power of the Holy Spirit. It's time to stop doing life in your wisdom and power. It's time to get plugged into the unlimited power source of the Holy Spirit. "Holy Spirit, come in power and might and fill your Church." Man's cry- God's gift.

-68-
The Holy Spirit Works in Us

The Holy Trinity: God the Father, God the Son, and God the Holy Spirit. Three in one. Simple to understand, right? He may not be easy to comprehend, but He is more real and active in our lives than ever. The Holy Spirit is at work worldwide, in the Church, and in the life of every believer. Have you ever sat down to ponder what the Holy Spirit does within each of our hearts?

- **First, the Holy Spirit enlightens the Christian mind.**

    First Corinthians 2:10: "For unto us God revealed them through the Spirit; searches all things, even the depths of God."

    Romans 12:2: "And do not be conformed to this world, but transformed by the renewing of your mind."

    Ephesians 4:23: "And that you be renewed in the spirit of your mind."

It is the business of the Holy Spirit to lift the veil Satan has put over our minds and to illuminate them so that we can understand the things of God. He does this as we read and study the Word of God, which the Holy Spirit has inspired.

- **Second, not only does the Holy Spirit enlighten the Christian's mind, but He also dwells in the physical body of every believer.**

  First Corinthians 6:19: "Do you not know that your body is a temple of the Holy Spirit who is in you, whom you have from God, and that you are not your own."

If we, as believers, rolled that truth over and over in our minds until we believed it, we would be far more careful about what we eat, drink, look at, or read.

  First Corinthians 9:27: "No, I beat my body and make it my slave so that after I have preached to others, I myself will not be disqualified for the prize."

The Holy Spirit works in you as a believer in Jesus Christ. Christ in you, the hope of glory, abides in you. He dwells in you! Let this truth come alive in you; the very presence of God sets up a homestead in our earthly body. There, He encourages comfort, guides convicts, and gives us everything we need to live a victorious life in Christ. I pray you can receive this truth today and know that God has not left us alone to figure everything out for ourselves. Walk in confidence because He enlightens our minds and indwells our bodies. What a privilege we have in Jesus. Thank the Lord for saving your soul and sending us the Holy Spirit.

-69-
Getting Out of the Funk

Have you ever been caught in the funk of life? In other words, are you stuck in the rut of life in your job, marriage, or just life in general? Have you lost all excitement when it comes to living, and you are just going through the motions, and nothing seems to make you truly happy? It is so bad that you can't stand to see other people around smiling and being so cheerful. We realize something is wrong within us, but we are so deep in the funk that we throw up our hands and roll over. We don't have the energy or want-to to do anything about it.

What about spiritually? Have you ever been in a spiritual funk? We all have been there at one time or another. We fall into a stale routine, get busy, and don't spend time with the Lord. Maybe you are there right now. How do we realize if we are there? If you are spiritually in a funk, you have no desire to read God's Word and never have time to pray. You go to church, but you would rather be somewhere else. When you go to church, you complain about what is wrong or what could be done better. You are constantly negative and never satisfied. If that describes you, you are covered up with the funk. You are embedded.

Here is my first question. Why is being in a spiritual funk so bad? God wants to show us so much and tell us so many things, but we are not ready to receive them. When you are in the funk, your focus is centered on you. You will not see the needs of others, and people definitely cannot see Jesus in you. My second question is this: what must occur to get out of this spiritual funk?

Psalm 4:1-3: "Answer me when I call to you, O my righteous God. Give me relief from my distress, be merciful to me, and hear my prayer. How long, O men, will you turn my glory into shame? How long will you love delusions and seek false gods? Know that the Lord has set apart the godly for himself; the Lord will hear when I call to him."

The first step to getting out of the funk is prioritizing prayer. We must take time to talk and listen to the Lord. We must understand that God hears our prayers and cares about every detail of our lives. In our prayer time, we must confess our sins and ask for His forgiveness and grace. Get rid of the baggage of sin and guilt. Receive His grace and begin to walk in freedom once again.

The second step to get out of the funk is to ask God to give you a thirst for more of Him. Ask Him to use you and give you a purpose. Ask Him to help you see the big picture for your life from His perspective.

Psalm 63:1-3: "O God, you are my God, earnestly I seek you; my soul thirsts for you, my body longs for you, in a dry and weary land where there is no water. I have seen you in the sanctuary and beheld your power and your glory. Because your love is better than life, my lips will glorify you."

The third step to escape life's funk is to hunger for His Word. Ask God for a greater desire for the Word of God.

Hebrews 4:12: "For the word of God is living and active. Sharper than any double-edged sword, it penetrates even to dividing soul and spirit, joint,

147

marrow, it judges the thoughts and attitudes of the heart."

I want to encourage you to maintain a good balance in life. Work hard and rest easy. Sometimes, it helps to get away, step away from the crazy-paced life, the busy schedule, and all your appointments. Ensure you receive more from the Lord than you are giving away. Don't hesitate to ask for help; talk with a godly friend. God bless.

-70-
Dealing With the Flesh

Genesis 3:6: "When the woman saw that the fruit of the tree was good for food and pleasing to the eye, and also desirable for gaining wisdom, she took some and ate it. She also gave some to her husband, who was with her, and ate it."

E ve desired to "gain wisdom"-Satan turned a healthy desire into an unhealthy decision. And Eve she disobeyed God. The flesh is the Bible's word for unperfected human nature. Self, at times, knows how to behave and be morally acceptable by most standards. But sooner or later, the self will be very selfish, always looking out for number one. We try hard to educate, train, and discipline ourselves, but the flesh seems to have a mind of its own.

Romans 7:18-19 Paul says, "I know that nothing good lives in me, that is, in my sinful nature. For I have the desire to do what is good, but I cannot carry it out. For what I do is not the good I want to do; no, the evil I do not want to do this I keep on doing."

Our flesh has a mind of its own; it is not subject to the law of God. God clearly says He has no confidence in our flesh, and Paul declared that he knew nothing good that dwells in him. When we realize this and yield to the Holy Spirit, greater victory, spiritual growth, love, peace, and joy will spring from our lives.

Psalm 37:4-7: "Delight yourself in the Lord and he will give you the desires of your heart. Commit your way to the Lord; trust him, and he will do this: He will make your righteousness shine like the dawn, the justice of your cause like the noonday sun. Be still before the Lord and wait patiently for him; do not fret when men succeed in their ways when they carry out their wicked schemes."

If we truly love God, we want to do what pleases Him. Delighting in the Lord alters the desires of selfishness. I want to encourage you to take the time to be still and know that He is God. Take time through the days to reflect on God's goodness and mercies. Praise Him for who He is and how much He loves us. Thank the Lord for the gift of the Holy Spirit.

-71-
Give Freely and Refresh Others

Whenever I need good, sound instruction, my go-to is the book of Proverbs. Proverbs were common to all the nations of the ancient world. This particular collection was made mainly by Solomon, in 1 Kings 4:32, who is said to have uttered three thousand proverbs. The overall theme of the book has to do with wisdom. I don't know about you, but I need all the wisdom I can get. Solomon doesn't mix words or try to talk way over your head, but he willingly shares with us simple truths that will make a difference in your life and the lives of others. Are you looking for a new direction or a more fulfilling way of life? Maybe you have achieved all your life goals but still feel empty. I challenge you to read through the book of Proverbs and ask God to give you wisdom and discernment. Read one chapter a day and complete the book in 31 days. Let's discover practical truths to help us make positive life changes.

> Proverbs 11:23-25: "The desire of the righteous ends only in good, but the hope of the wicked on in wrath. One man gives freely yet gains even more; another withholds unduly, but comes to poverty. A generous man will prosper; he who refreshes others will himself be refreshed."

The world will read this and laugh in our faces. This scripture is the opposite of what we will hear from earthly wisdom. This world will tell you that if you want to be fulfilled and happy, you must work long hours, make sacrifices, and do whatever it takes to climb the ladder of success. Some of the rich people of our time put all their energy into climbing the ladder of success, and when they got to the top, they found out they had climbed the wrong ladder. They discovered that money and success don't bring happiness and meaning; you only want more, which doesn't satisfy you.

I want to challenge you today to open your eyes and notice the people around you. Listen to what they say and see their needs, Then give generously. The man who gives freely will gain even more. This is a promise from the Word of God; you can bank on this truth. That may sound backward, but be willing to trust God in His Word. Then, ask the Lord how you can refresh others. There is so much discouragement and depression in our world today, and we all need a word of encouragement. Make it a priority to speak words of encouragement to others daily. Be intentional with your comments and pour out encouragement and grace to those overwhelmed. God's Word says it will come back to you many times over. Give generously and refresh others; it will make you smile. May the Father's Grace and Peace be multiplied to you and your family.

More Books By Dennis Taylor

1. **Fuel For Today:** A 6-Month Devotional Guide For Spiritual Growth And Encouragement
2. **The Total Package:** The Balanced Life
3. **Fuel For Today Volume 2:** A 3-Month Devotional Guide For Spiritual Growth And Encouragement.
4. **Surrendered:** From Stressed To Blessed; Your Best Life In Jesus' Easy Yoke
5. **He Fills My Cup:** A 90-Day Devotional To Refresh And Restore Your Soul; Drink From The Fountain.
6. **Say It Again:** For The Ones On The Front Row
7. **Temptation In Seven Stages**
8. **Sit Down At His Table:** A 6-Month Devotional Guide For Spiritual Growth And Encouragement
9. **Man Up:** Man's search for meaning.

Dennis L Taylor

About the Author

I started in Student Ministry when I was twenty years old, and it has been my calling for nearly thirty years. My heart was for students to come to know Christ and to grow in their relationship with Him. I love to see God's light bulb fill their eyes and hearts, and I loved sharing the Gospel of Jesus with students whom everybody else said were a lost cause. My passion was to teach them about a relationship with the Lord and give them a real-life example of what it looked like to be walked out in everyday life. My time alone with God has always been my rock, fortress, and high tower. Spending time praying each morning, reading God's Word, and listening to His voice has changed my life forever. I love sharing with young believers who dare to dive deep into the river of God's love. Investing in other people's lives is so rewarding, watching them go from the shallow end of faith and dive into the deep water of a love relationship with Jesus.

I had the privilege of pastoring two churches, a great blessing to my family and me. First, the Lord led us to plant a church in Leesburg, Georgia. It was a time of growth and a time of great joy. I loved preaching God's Word weekly and encouraging and loving families. We started with twelve people in our home one Sunday morning; a short time later, God opened the door to purchase a building on a couple of acres in Lee County. That church is still going strong and is known as Forrester Community Church. I also had the privilege of pastoring Salem Baptist Church in Worth County, Georgia. Salem is a small country church with a huge heart for God and its community. I was there briefly, but they have a special place in my heart.

Today, I serve as the Pastor of Sports and Recreation at Park Avenue in Titusville, Florida. Peter Lord was the founding pastor of Park Avenue Baptist Church. He was also the author of several well-known books such as Hearing God, Soul Care, 959 Plan, and many more. In addition, he was one of the greatest communicators of God's Word I have ever heard. As the Senior High Student Pastor, I was honored to be discipled by this great man of God in 2004. My role today at Park Avenue is to use sports and recreation to reach out to the community around us. As we develop relationships through sports, God opens the door to share our Jesus with them and their families. My hope, joy, and calling are to lead as many people as possible into a saving relationship with Jesus. Then, please encourage them to take those next steps to grow and mature in their faith.

In 2022, I wrote two devotional books, *Fuel for Today Volumes One and Two*. I also penned the book *The Total Package*, which deals with living a balanced life in Christ. My last books were *"Say It Again, Surrendered, and Man Up."* My previous devotionals are *He Fills My Cup and Sit Down At His Table*. Last but not least, I married Laura, my high school sweetheart, and we have been happily married for 36 years. The Lord has blessed us with two grown kids; Carsen serves in the Children's ministry at Passion City Church in Atlanta, Georgia. Mackenzie just got married and is currently working in Augusta, Georgia.